BLOOMS

COLORING BOOK

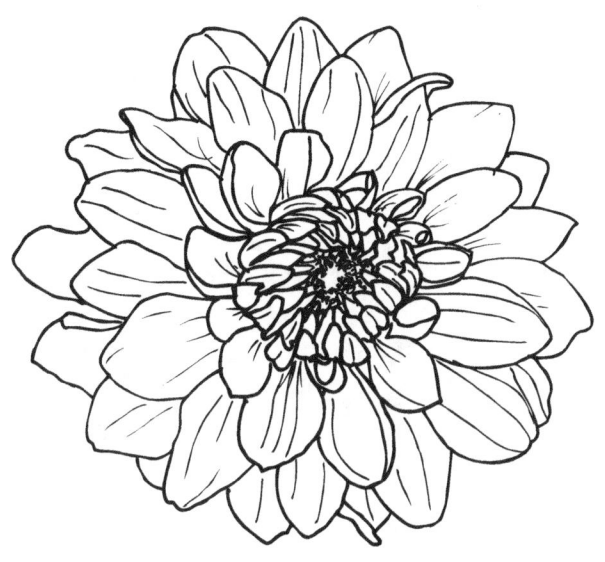

VOLUME 1

This book is printed on just one side of the paper
to avoid bleed through.

To view samples of these illustrations colored by the author please visit
www.lovelyleisure.me

LOVELY LEISURE

ILLUSTRATIONS BY PAULA PARRISH

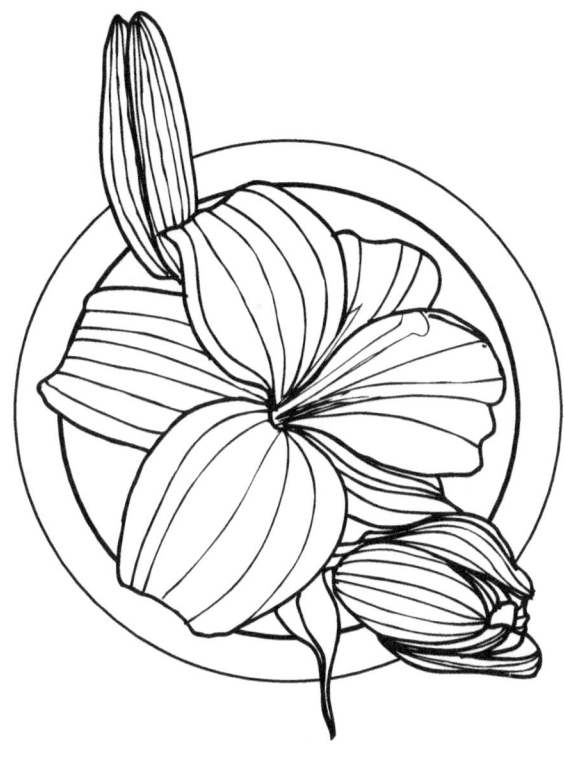

Blooms Coloring Book, Volume 1
© 2014 Paula Parrish

www.lovelyleisure.me

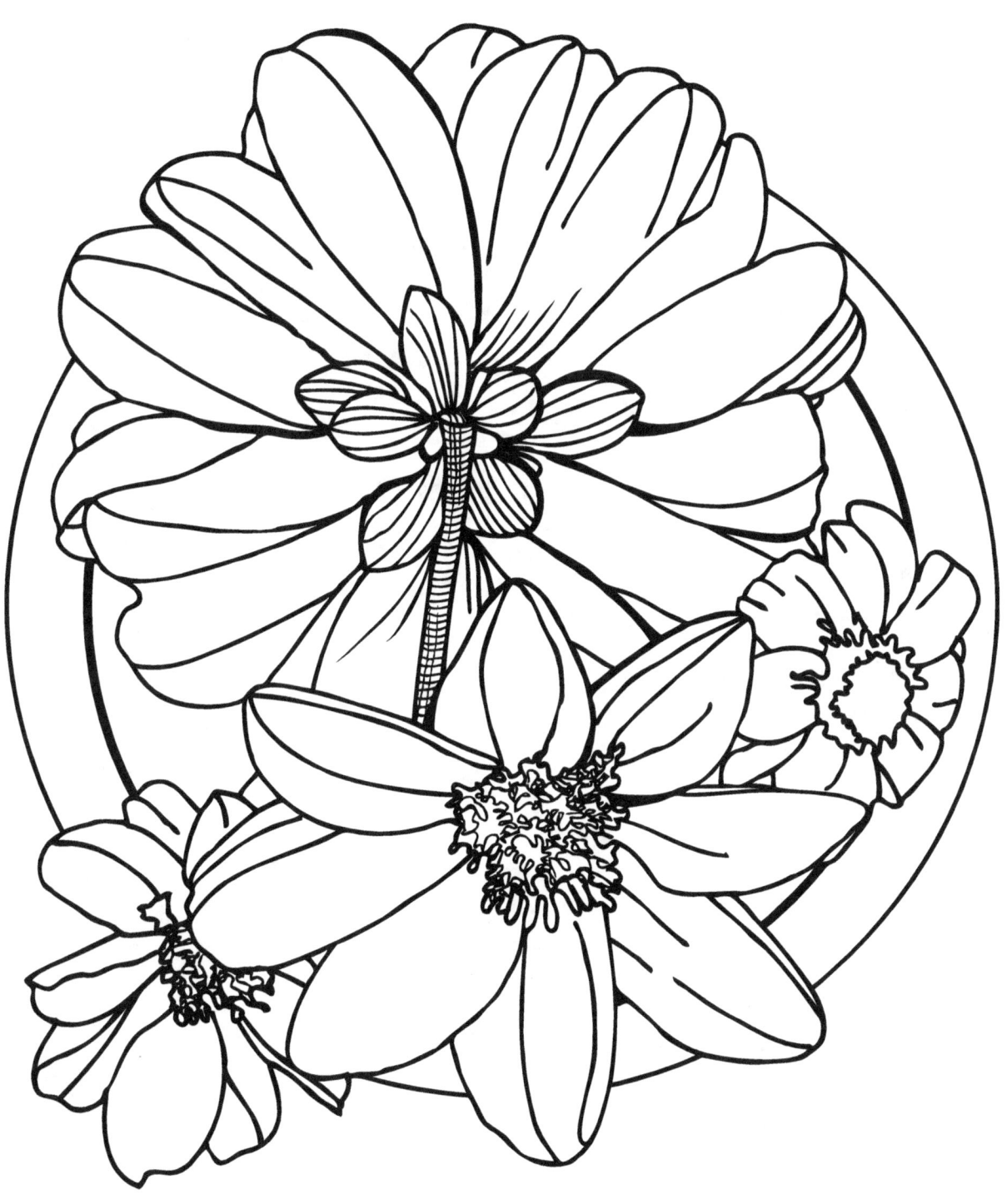

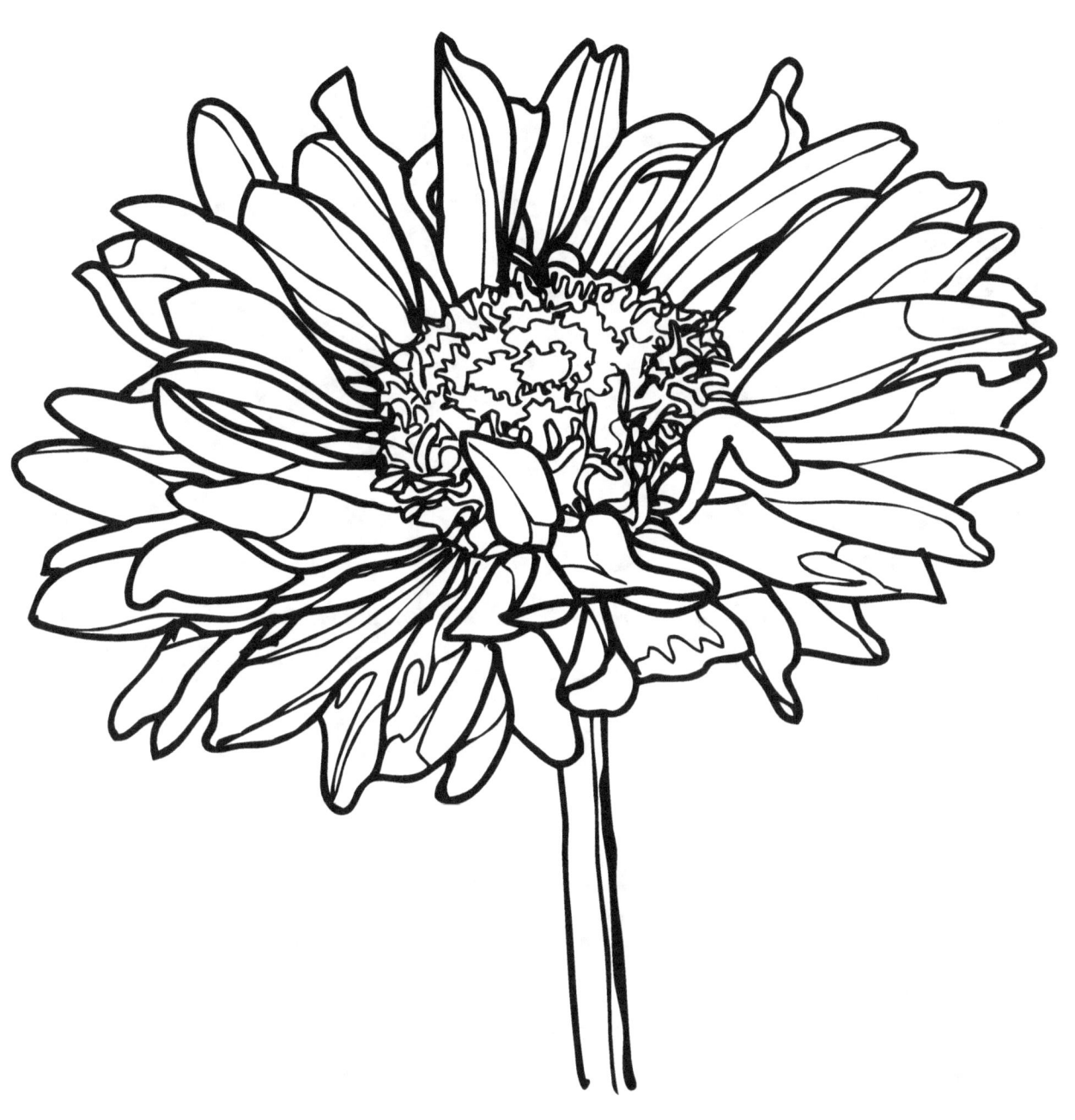

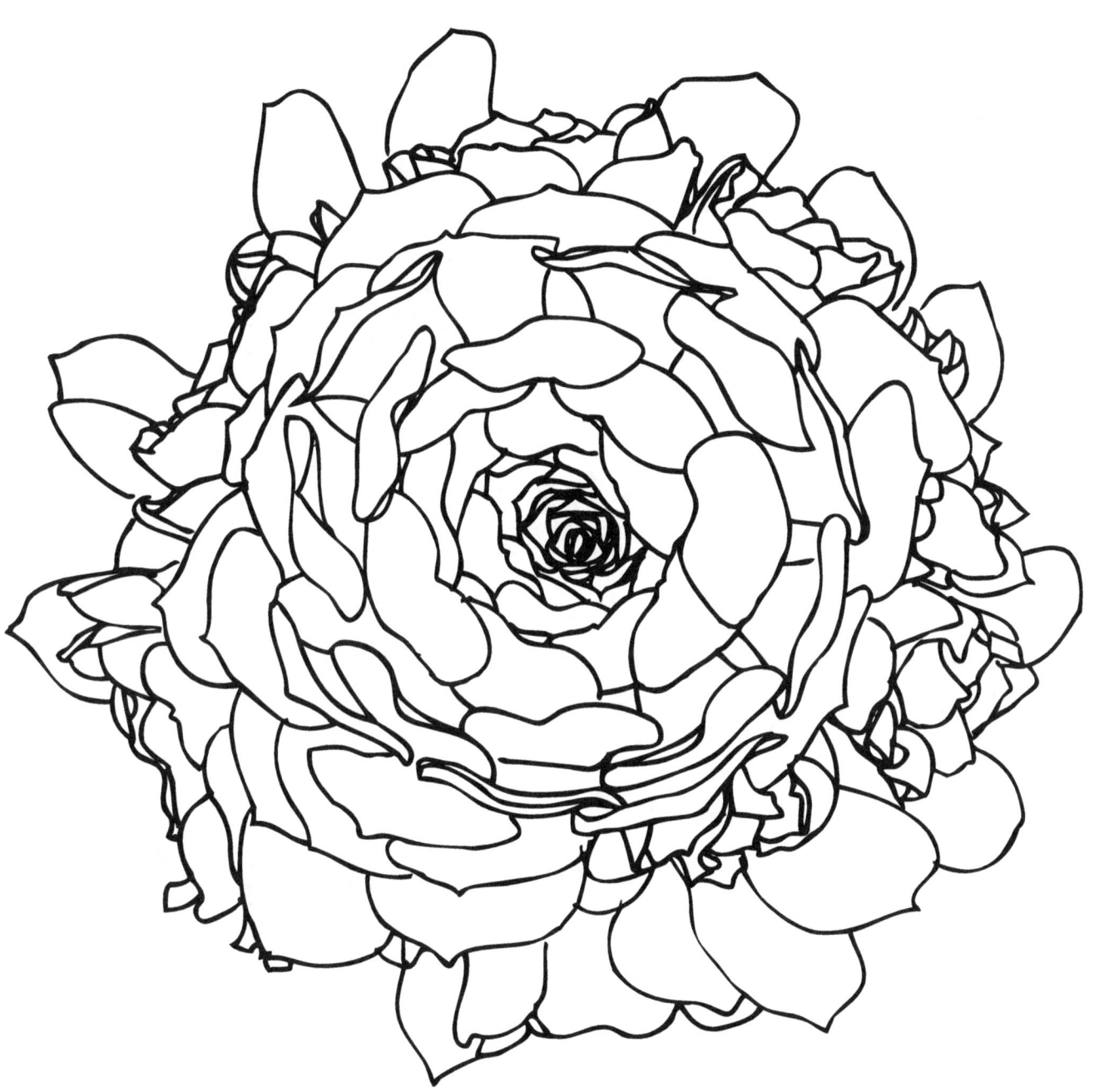

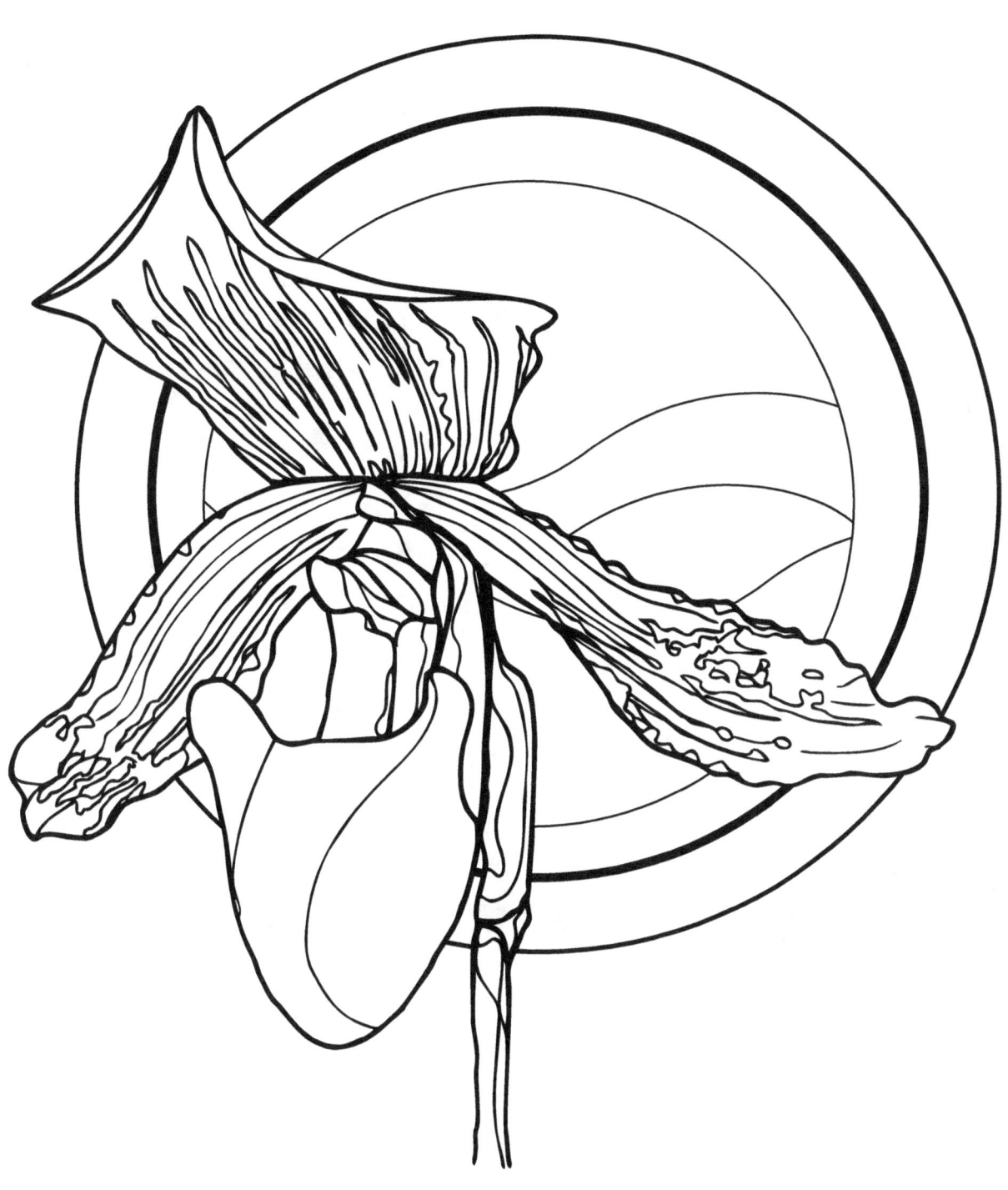

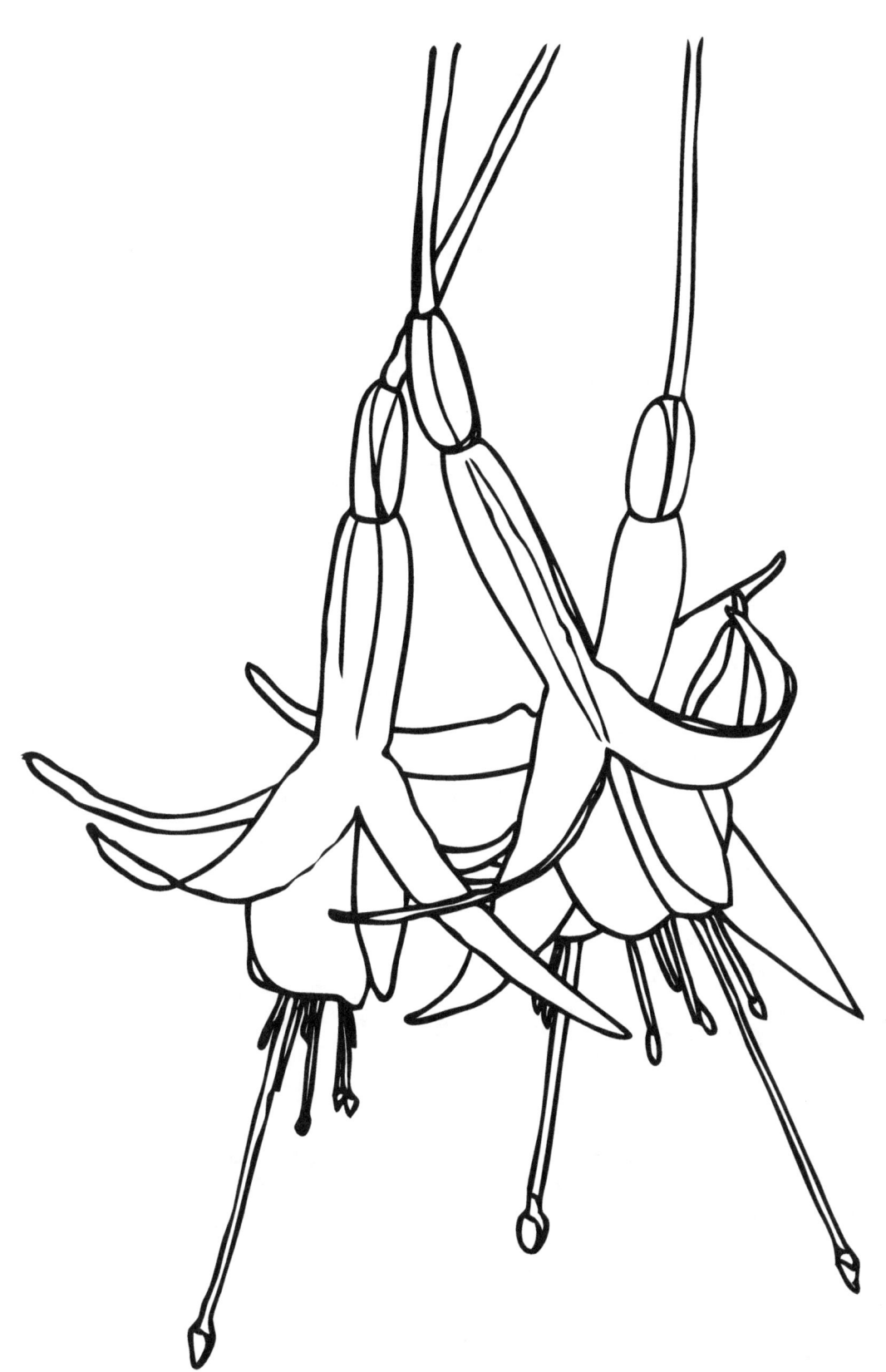

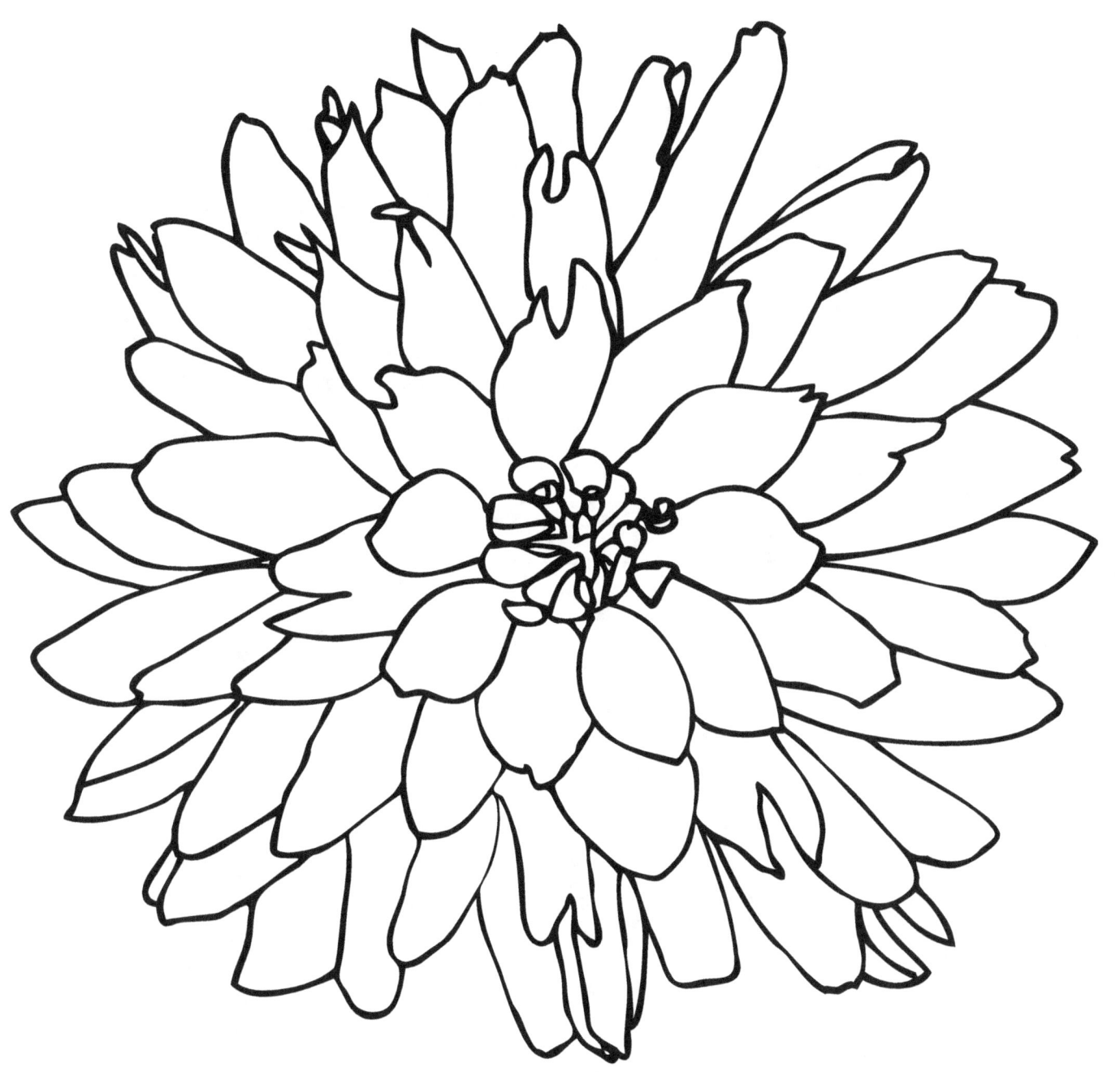

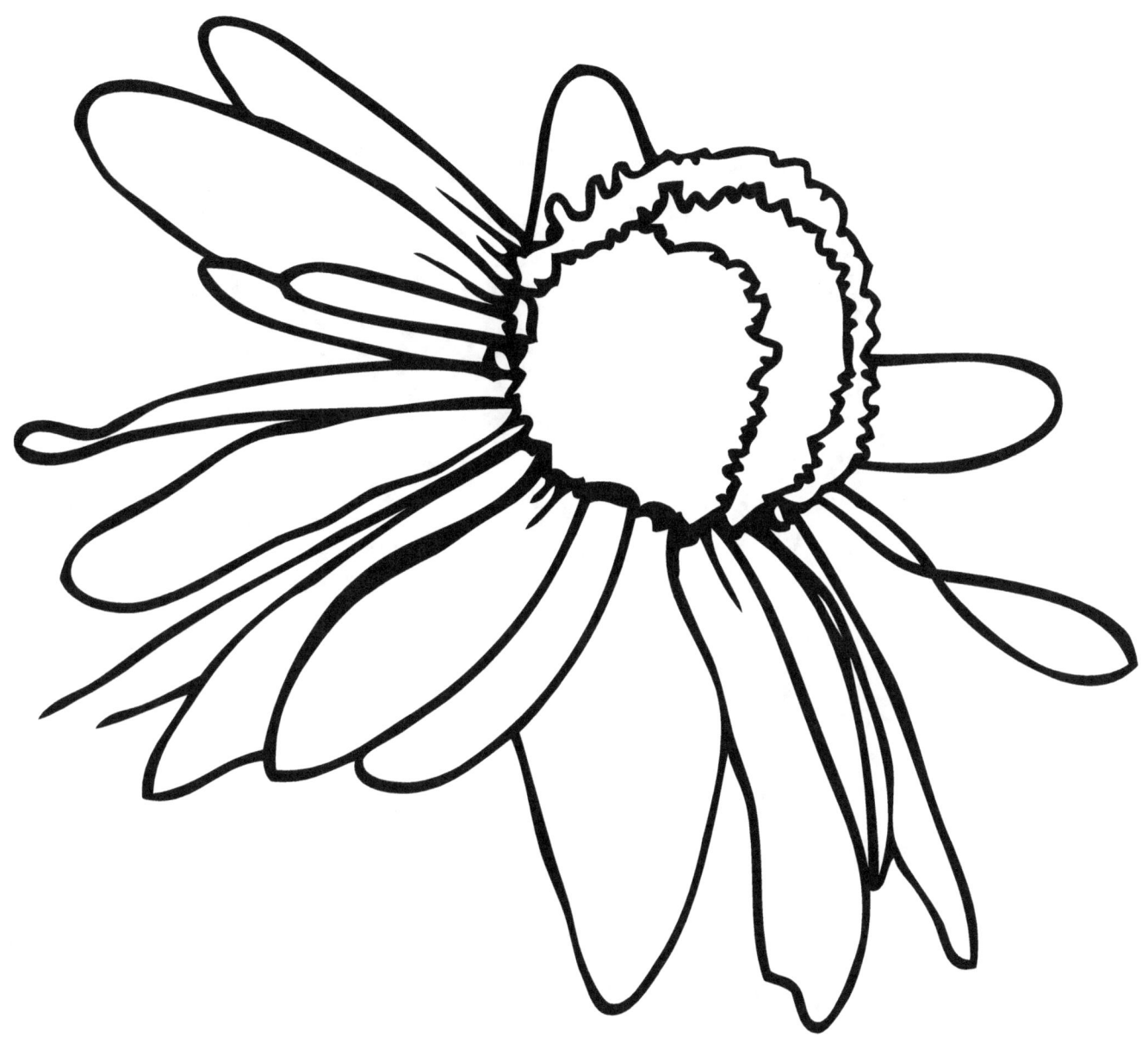

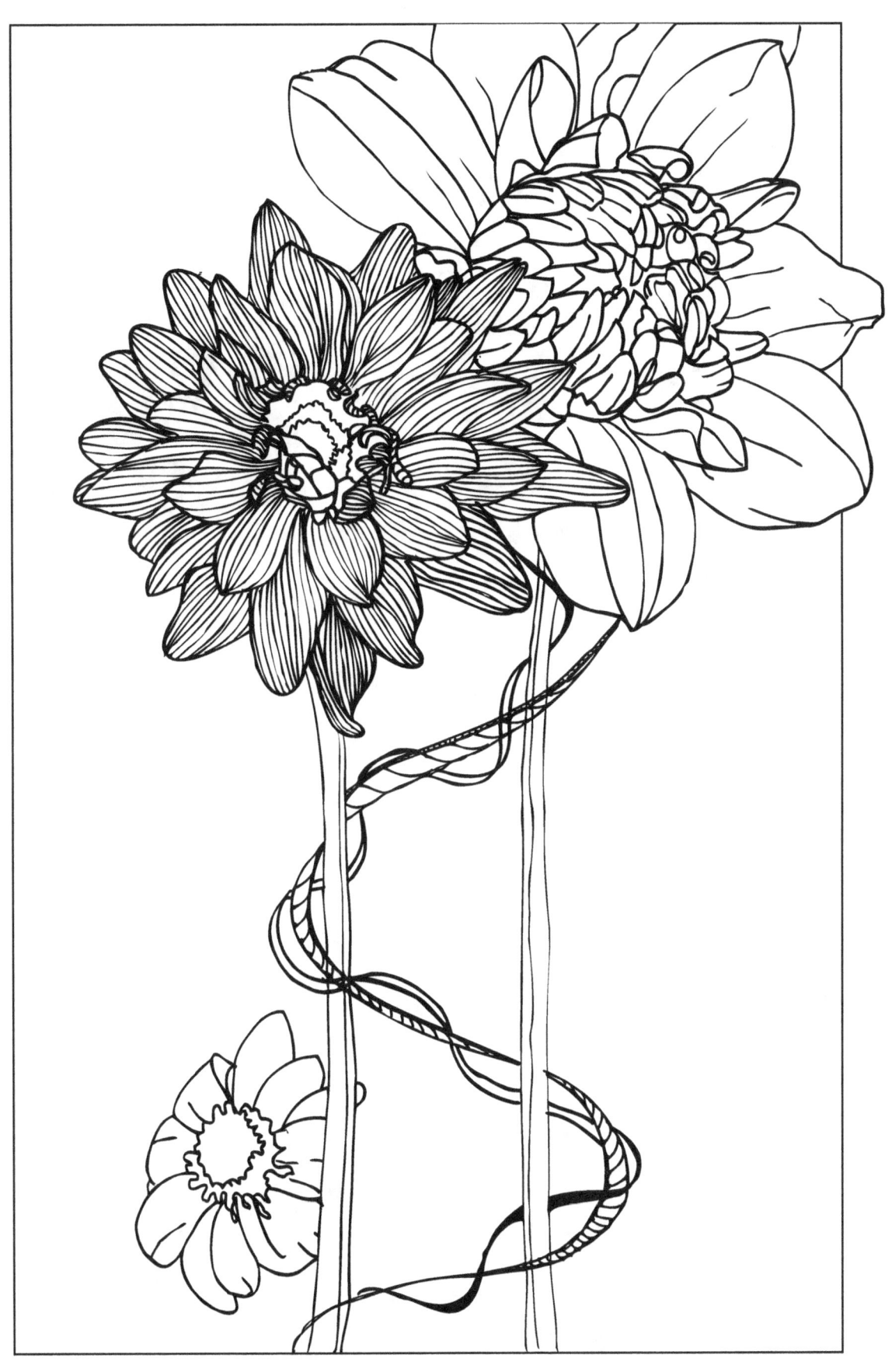

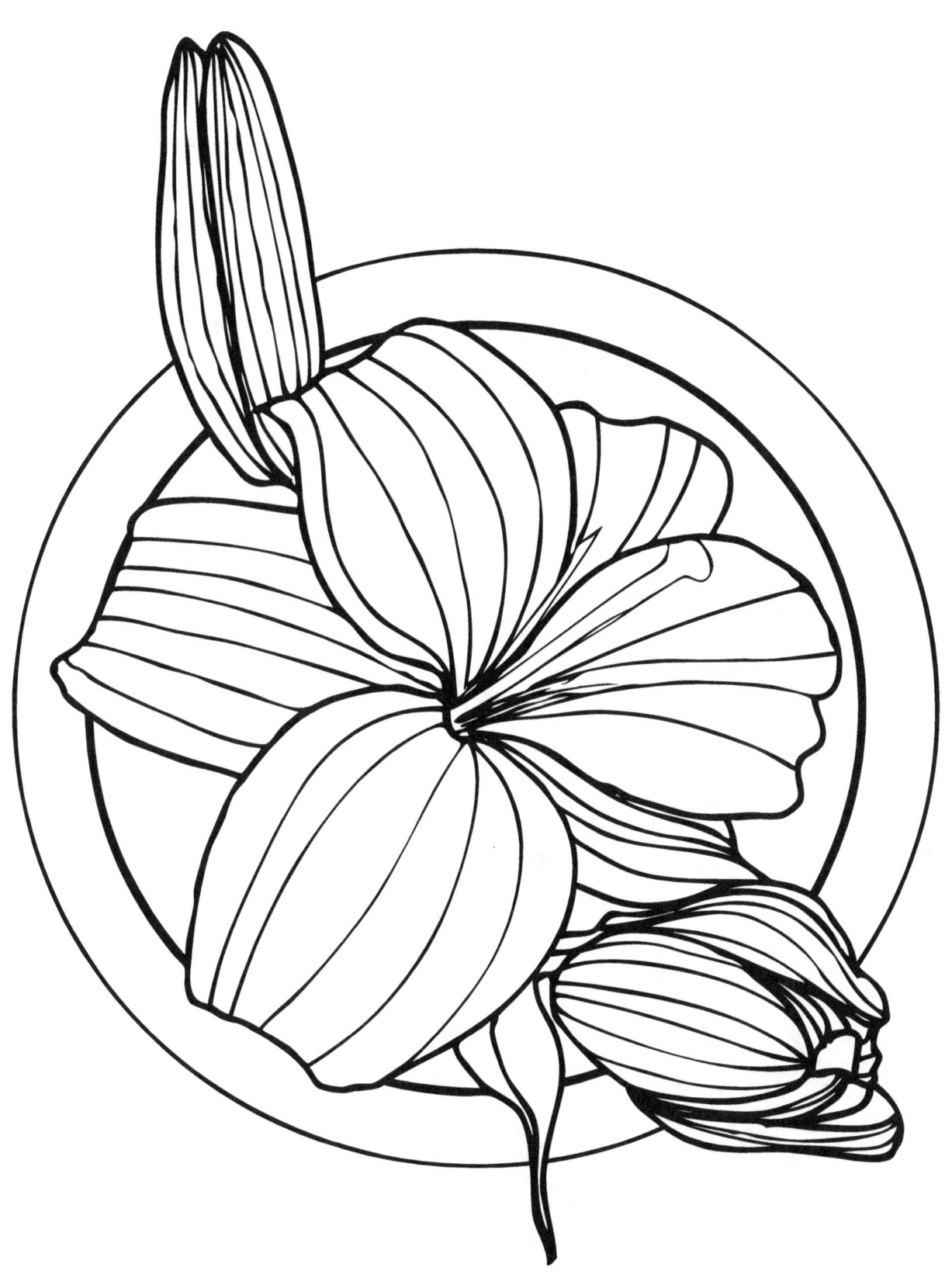

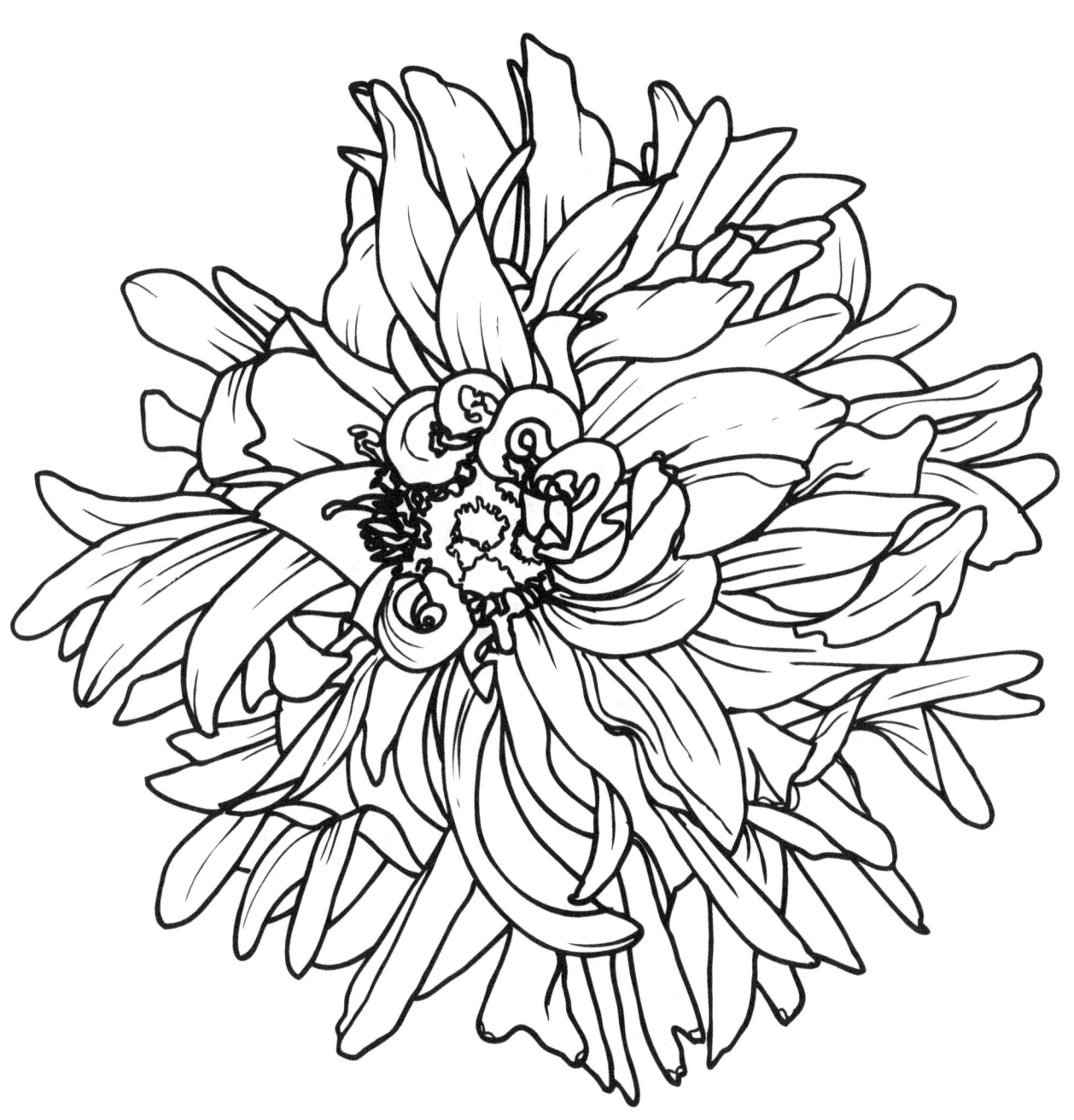

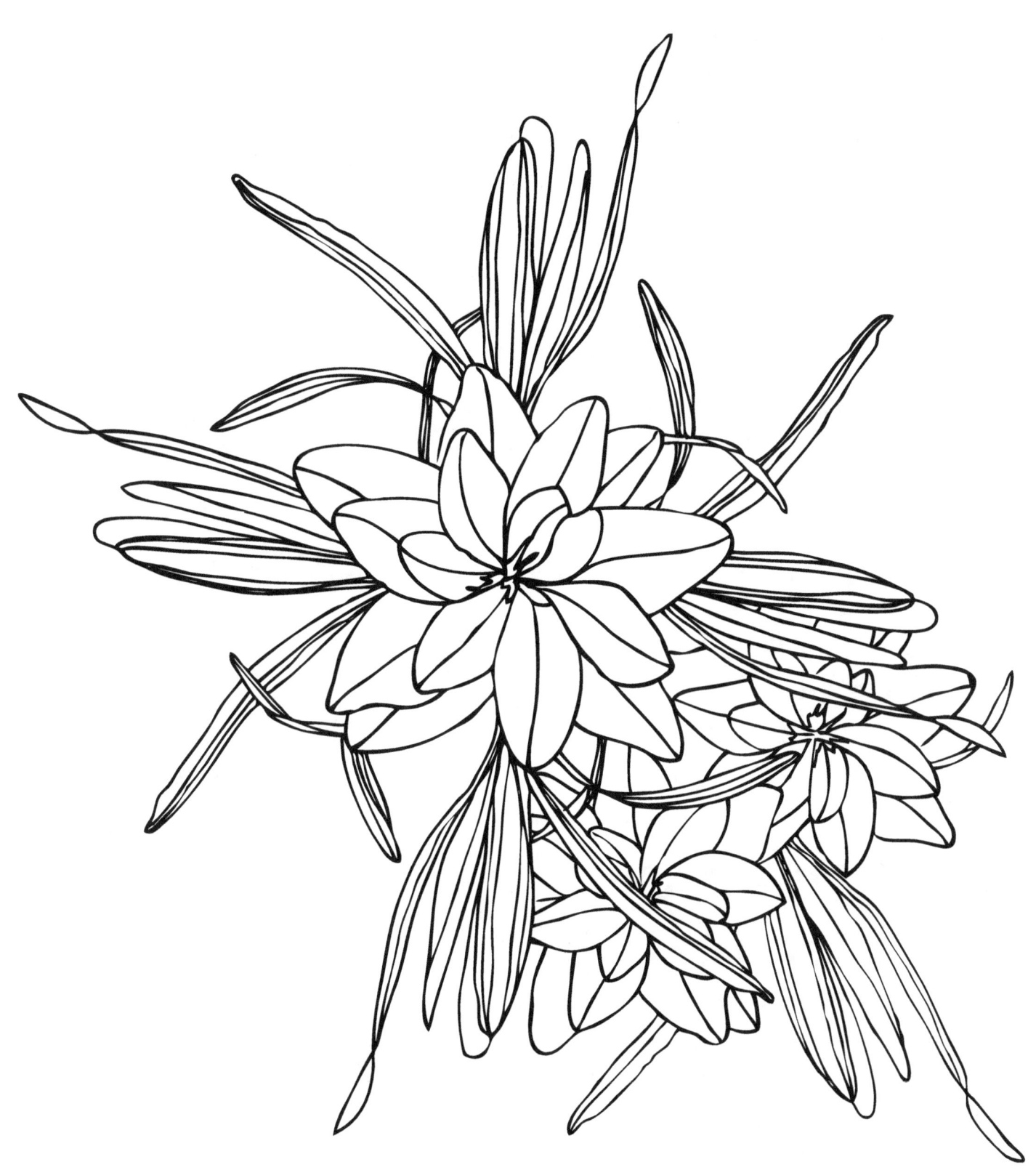

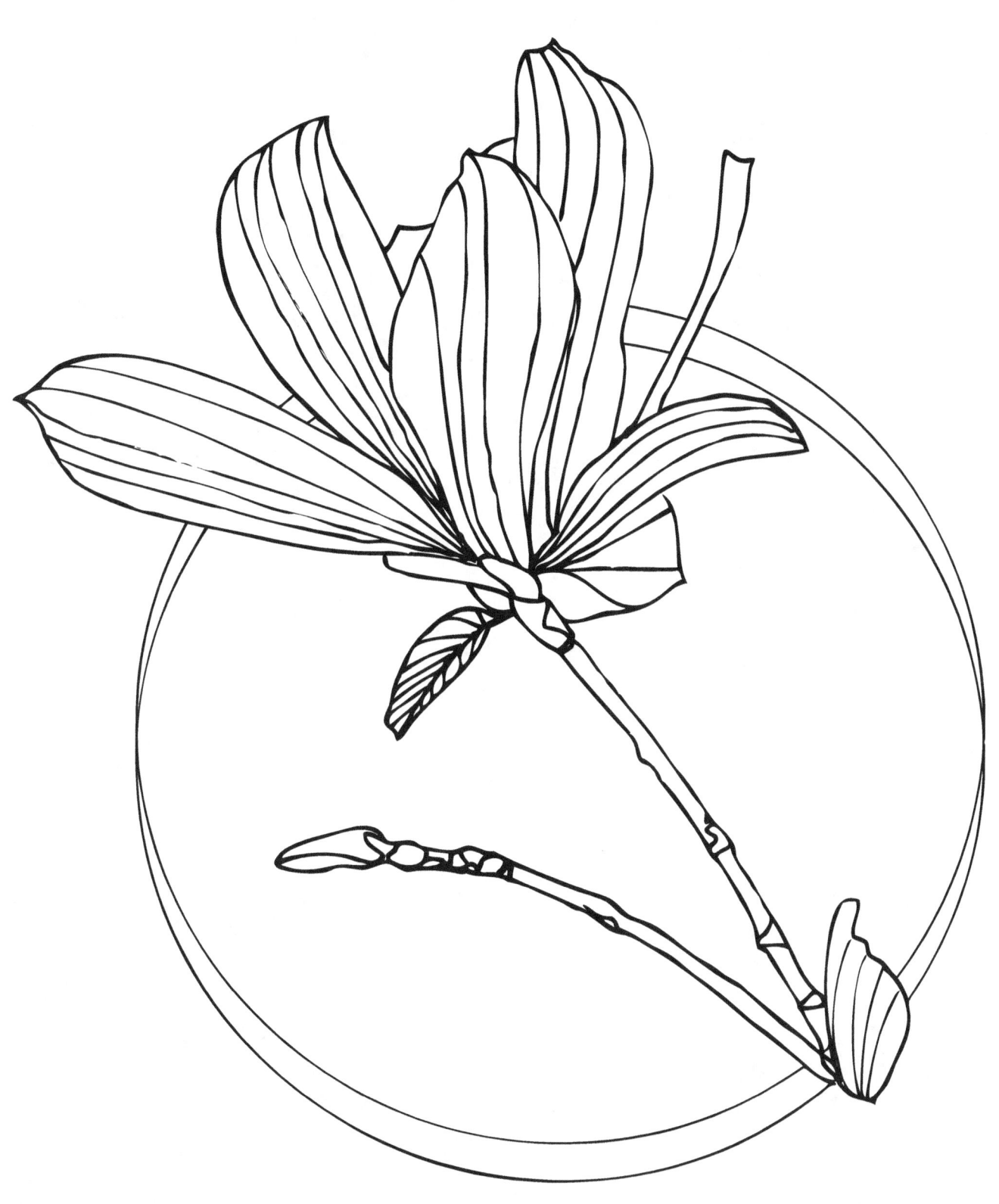

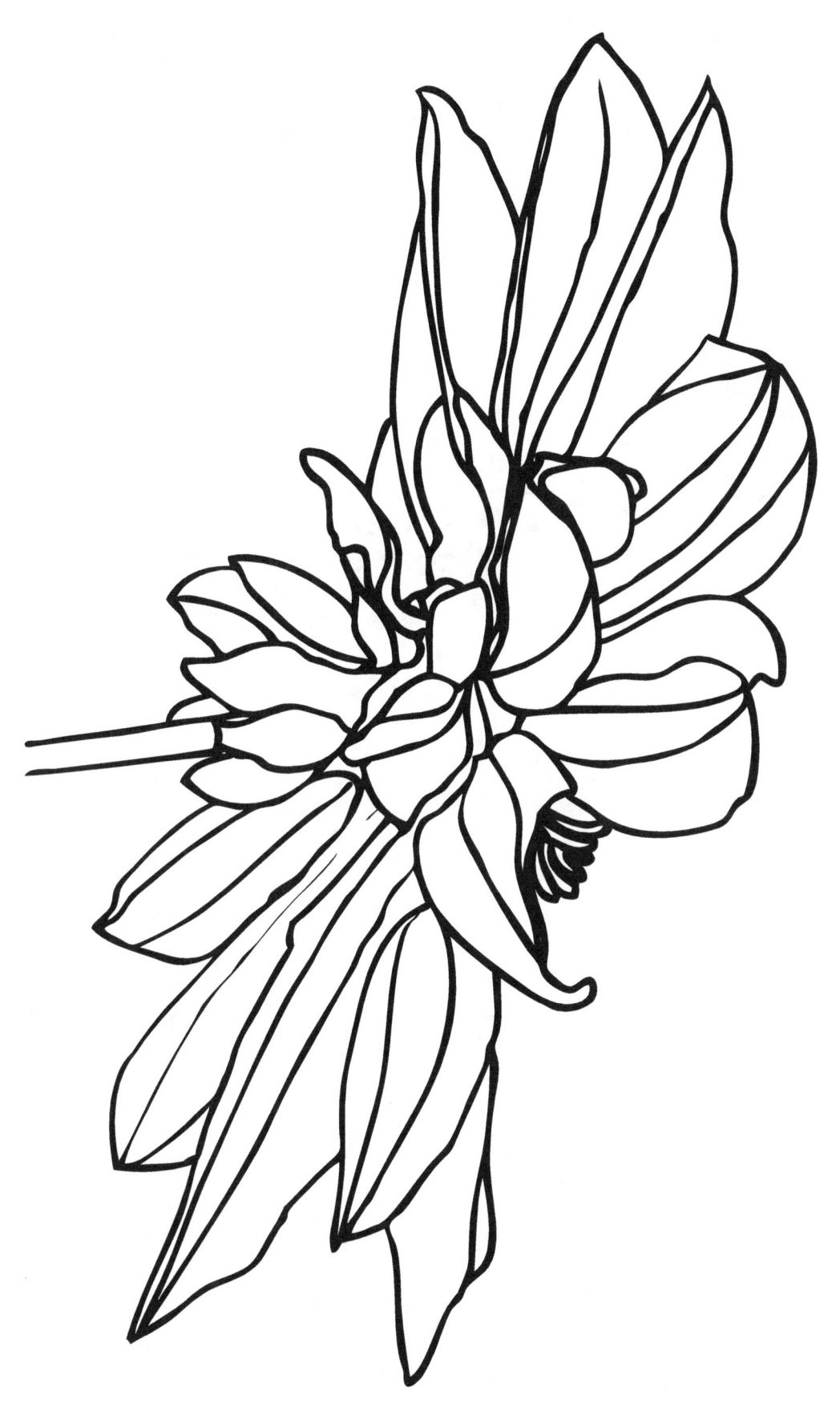

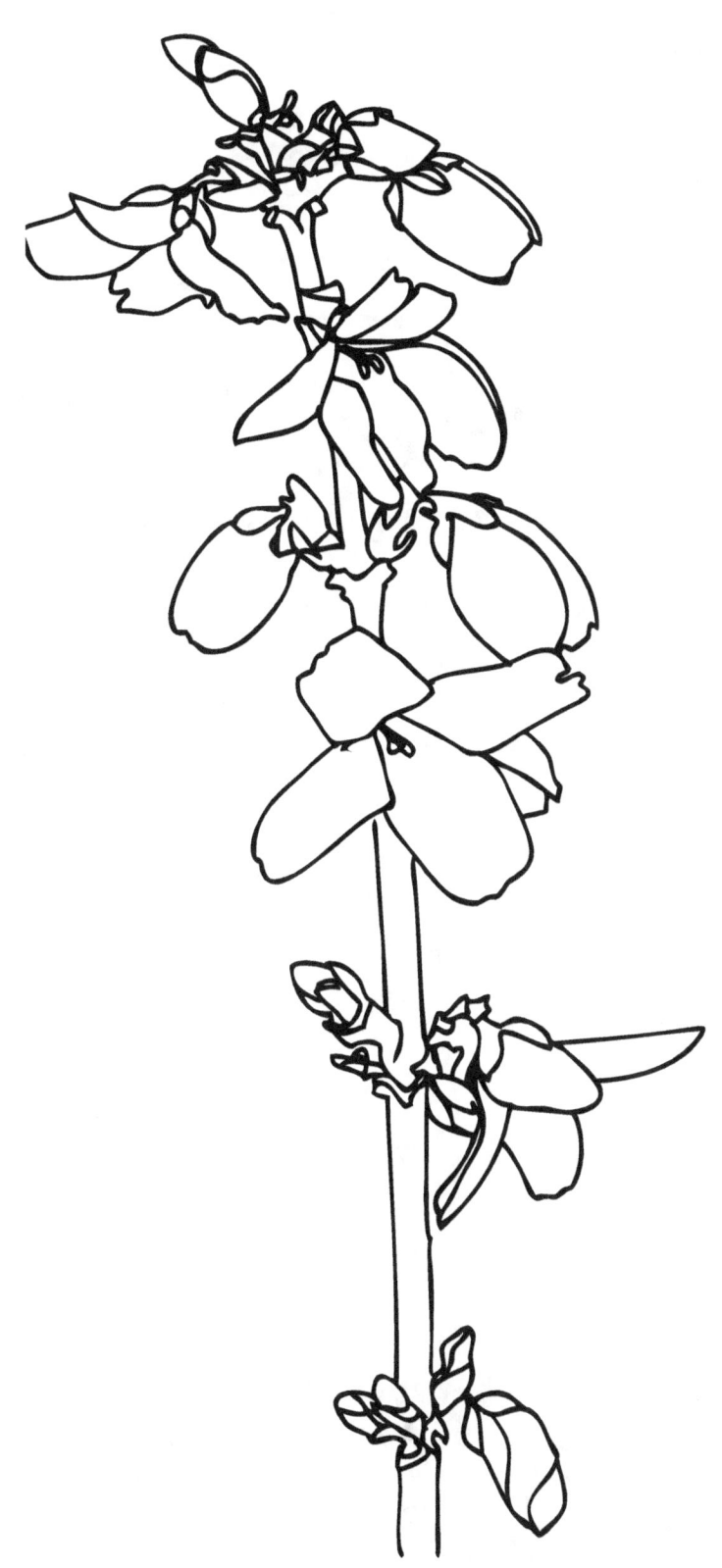

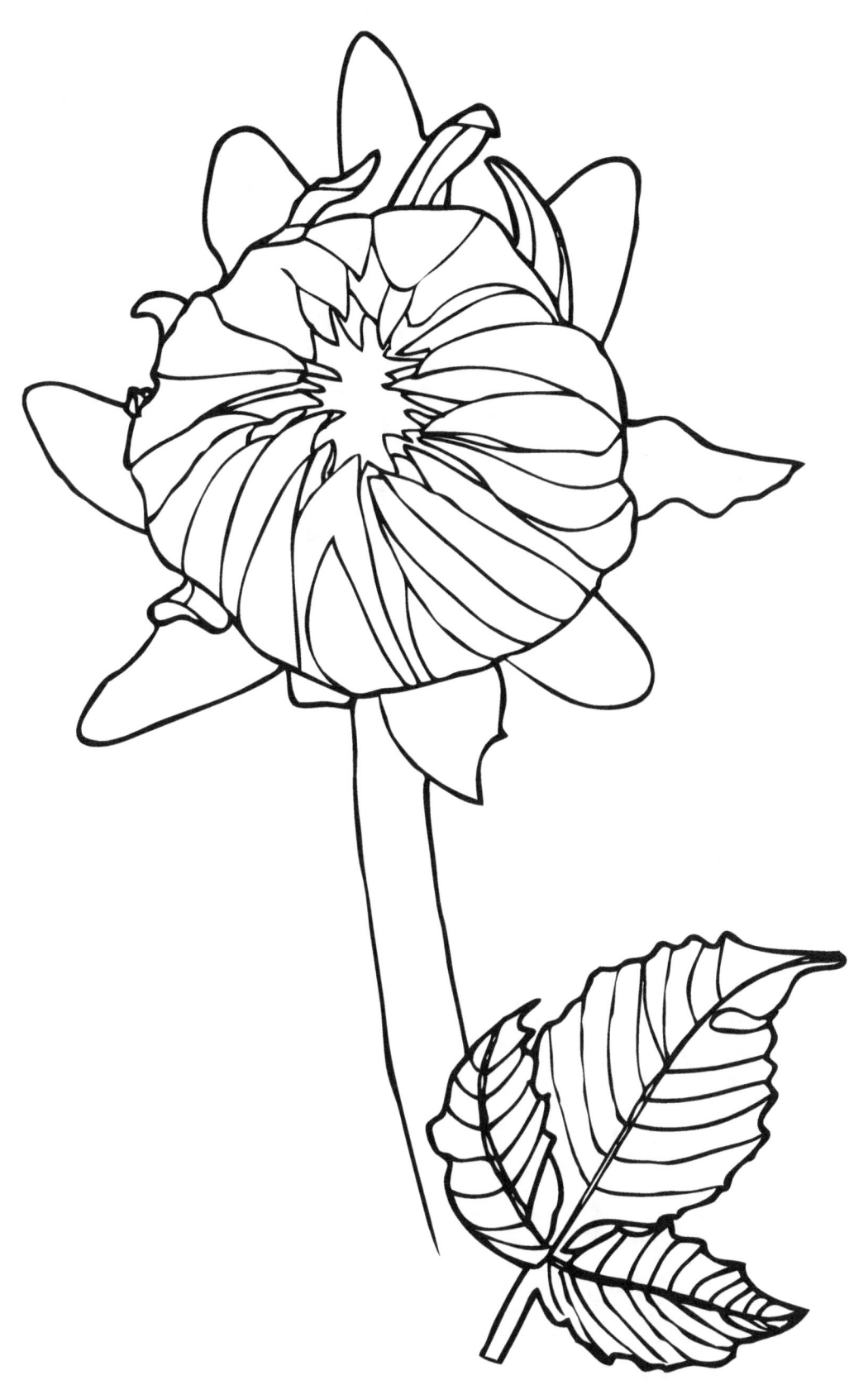

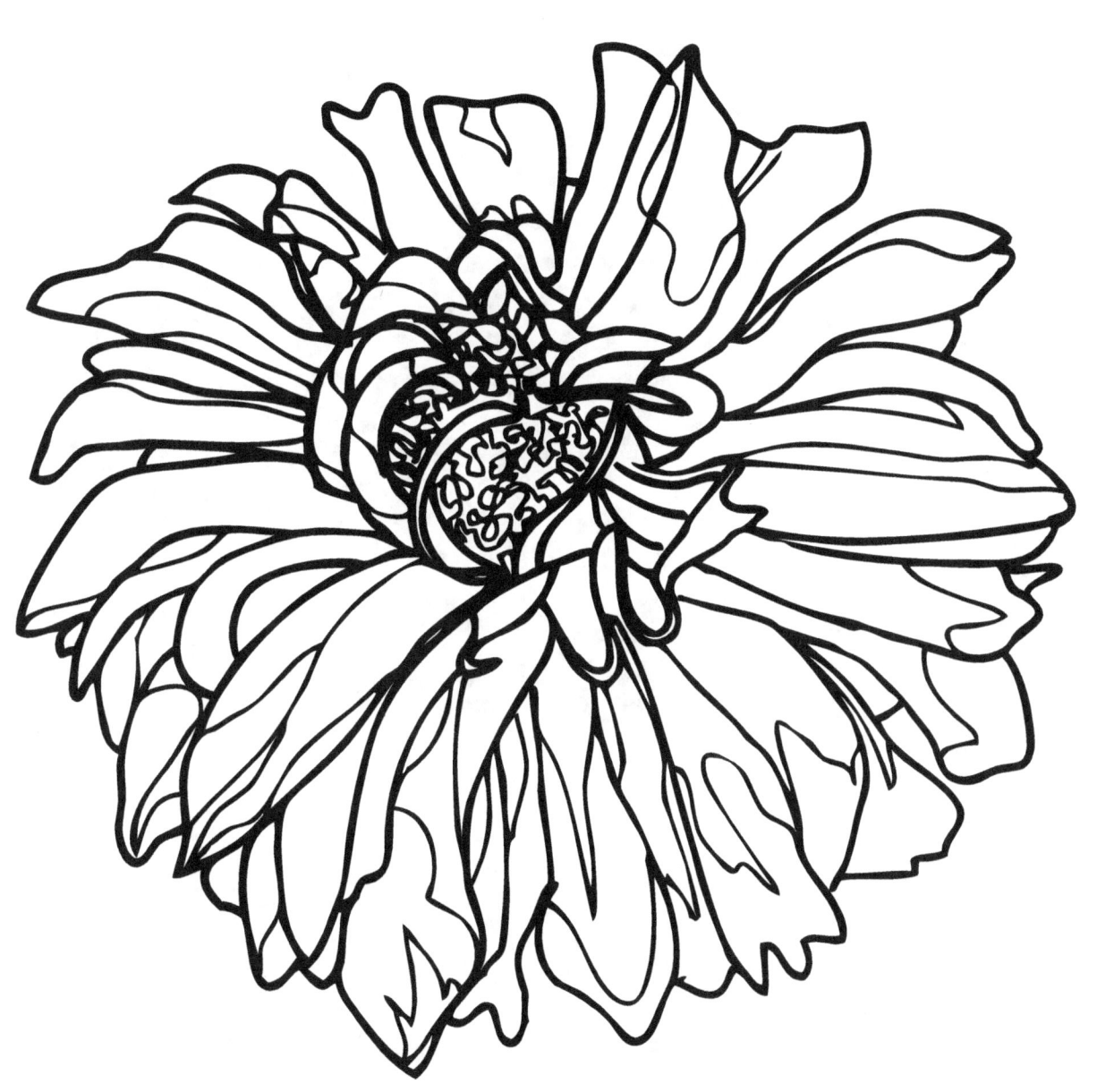

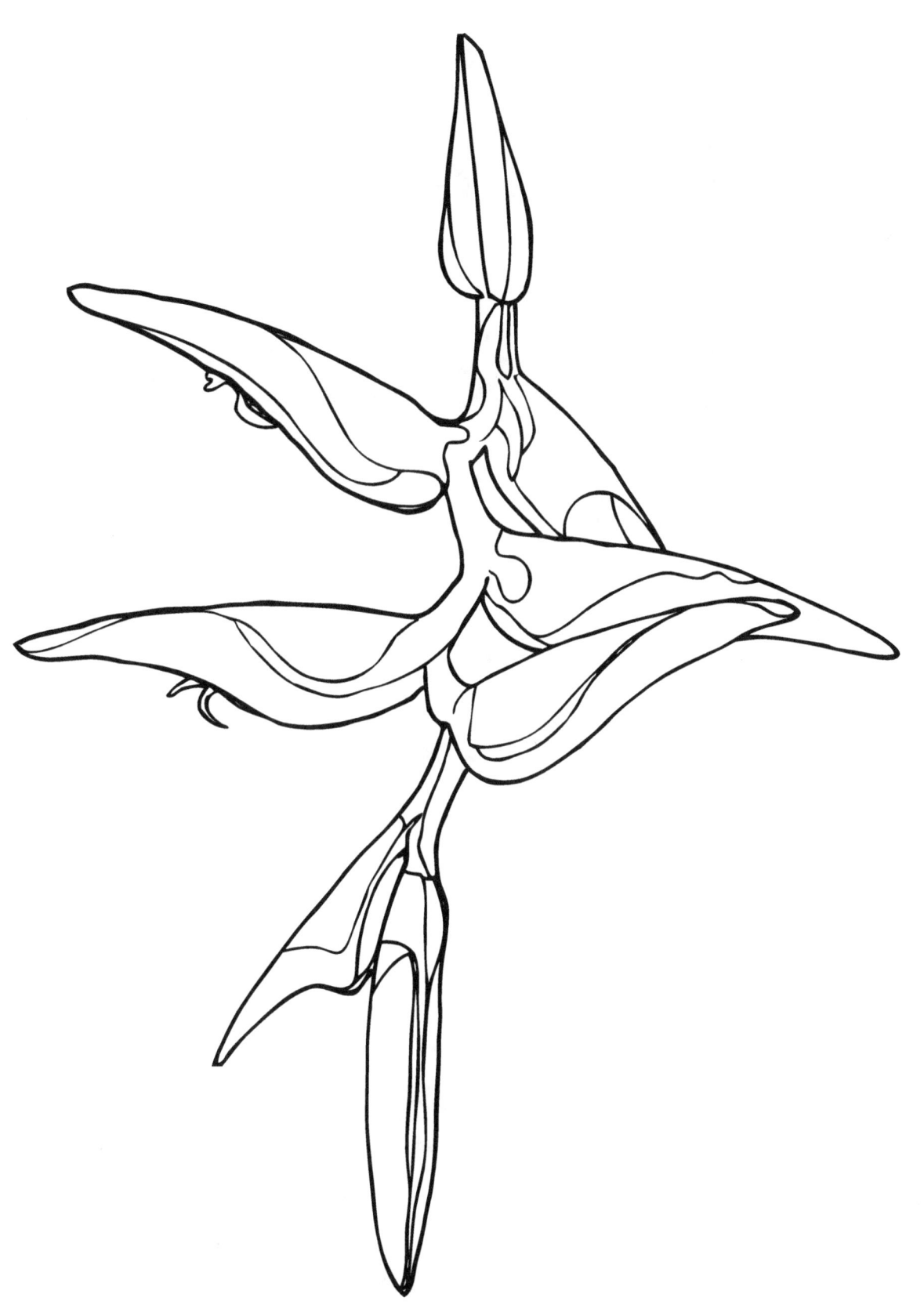

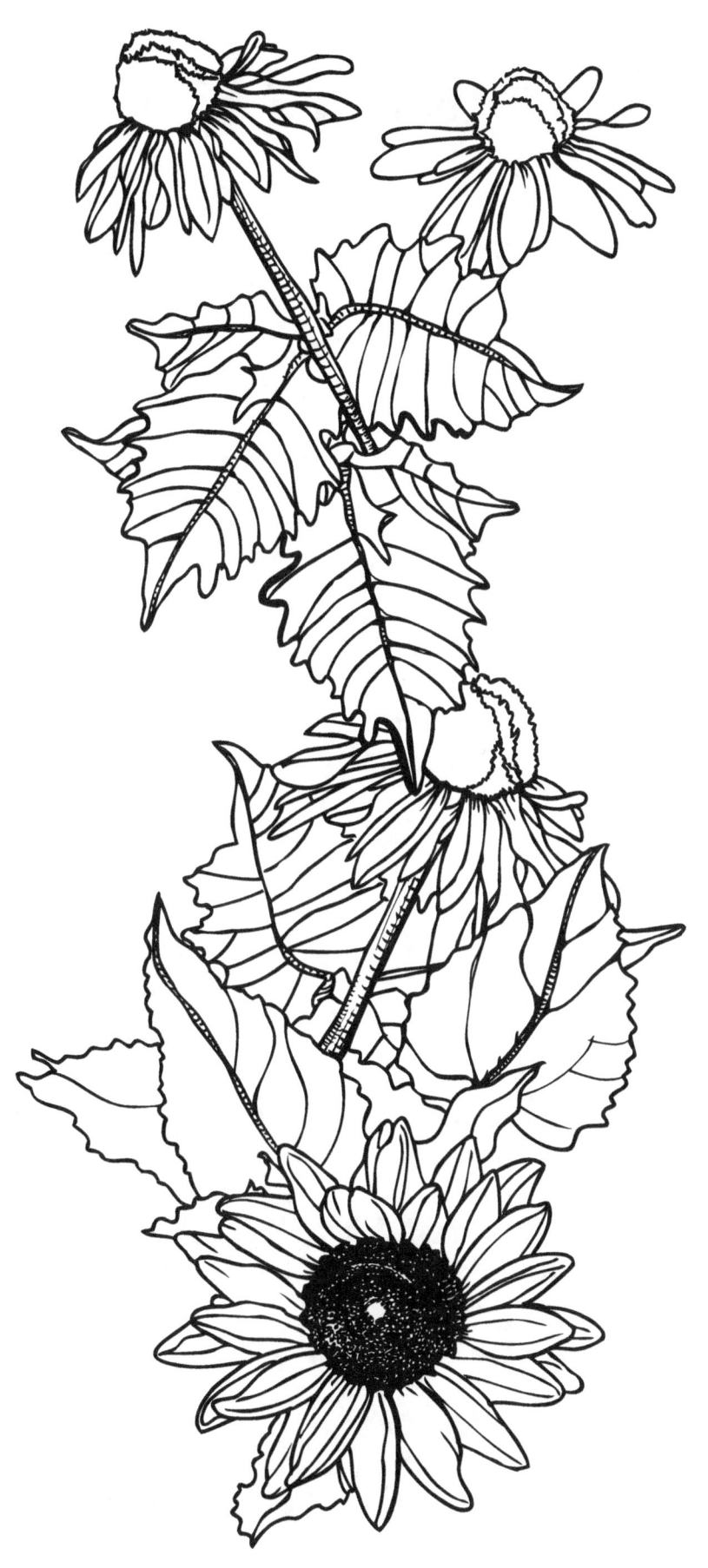

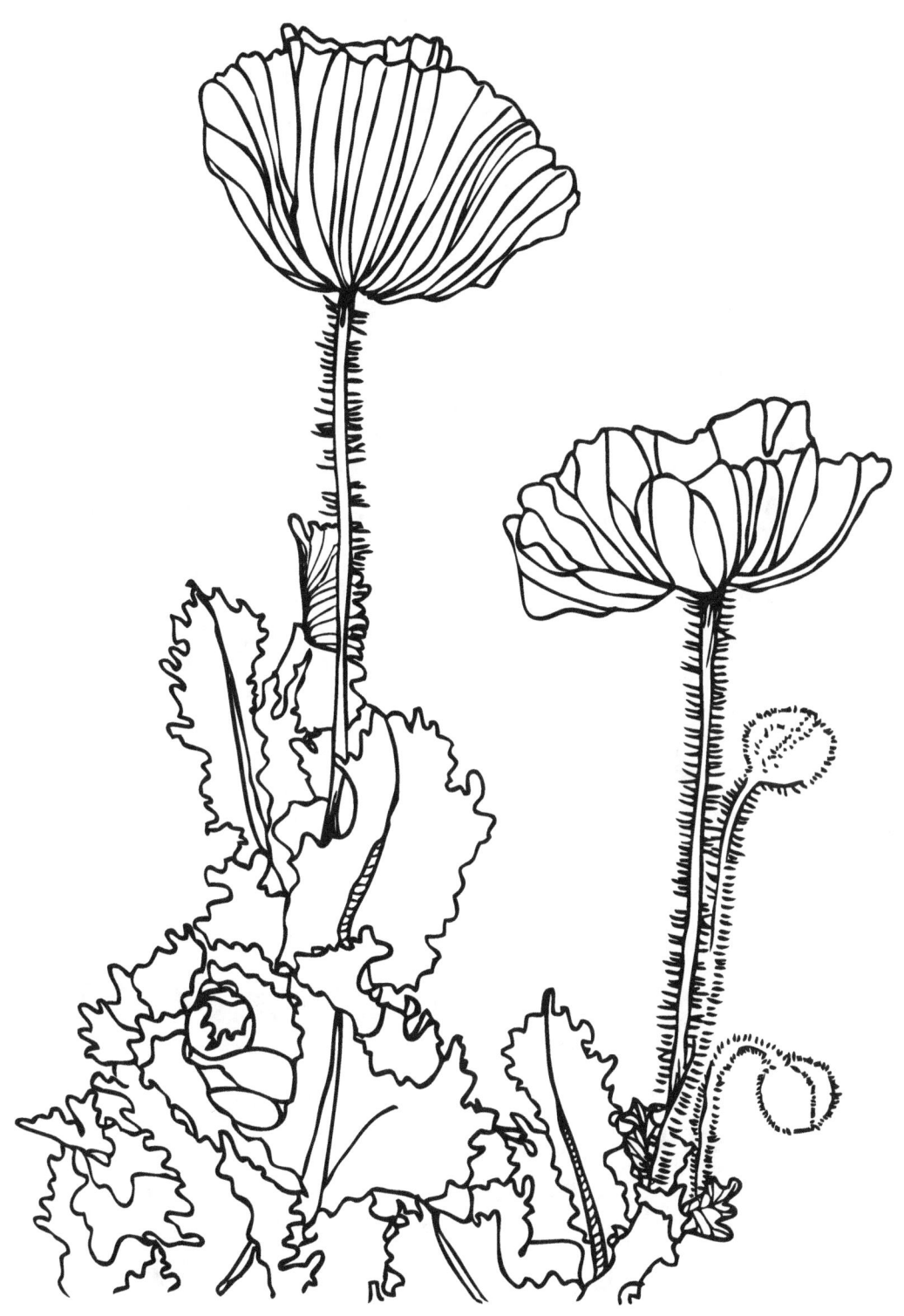

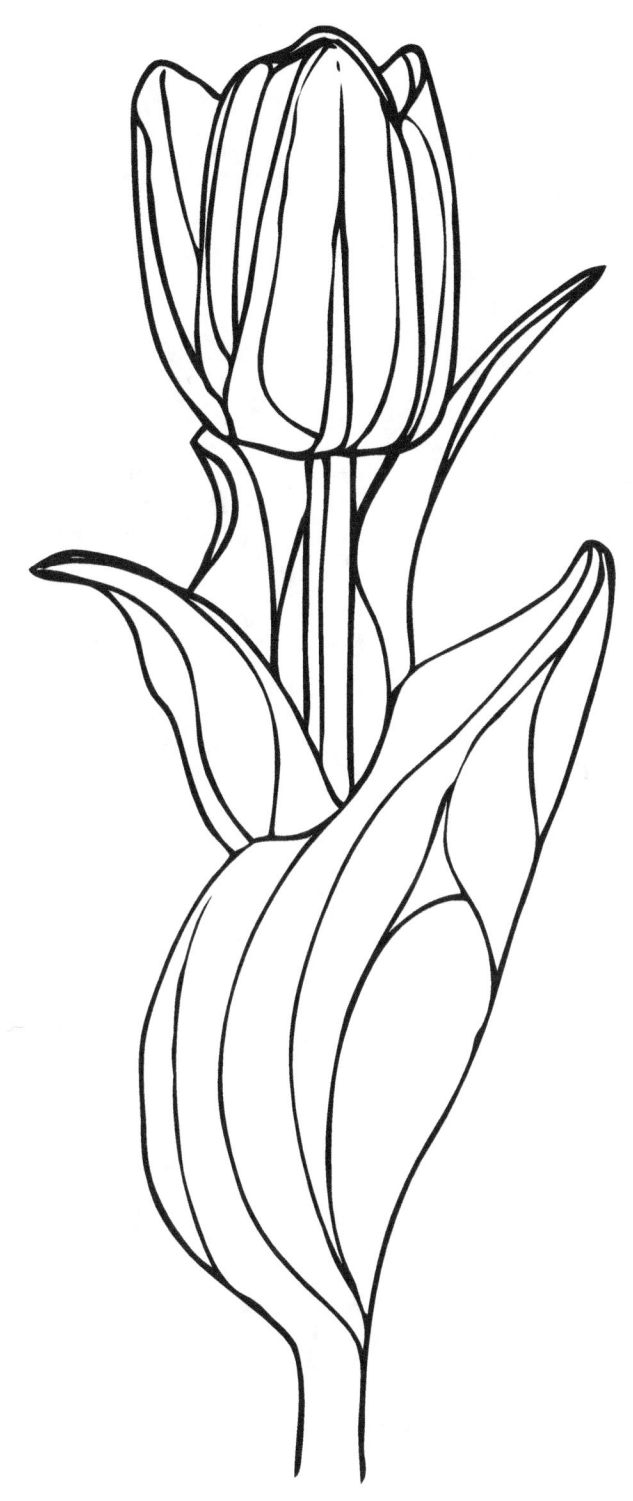

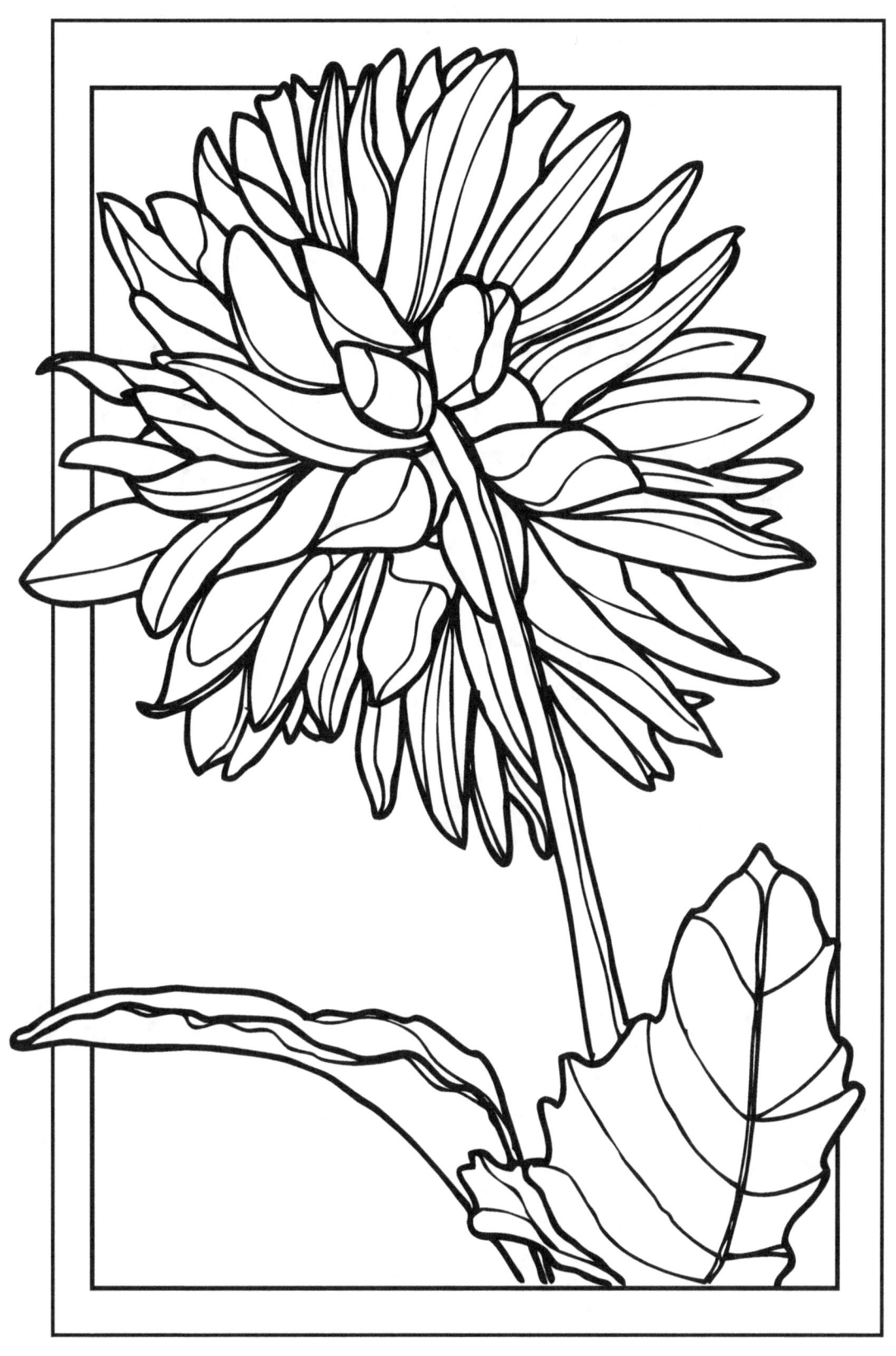

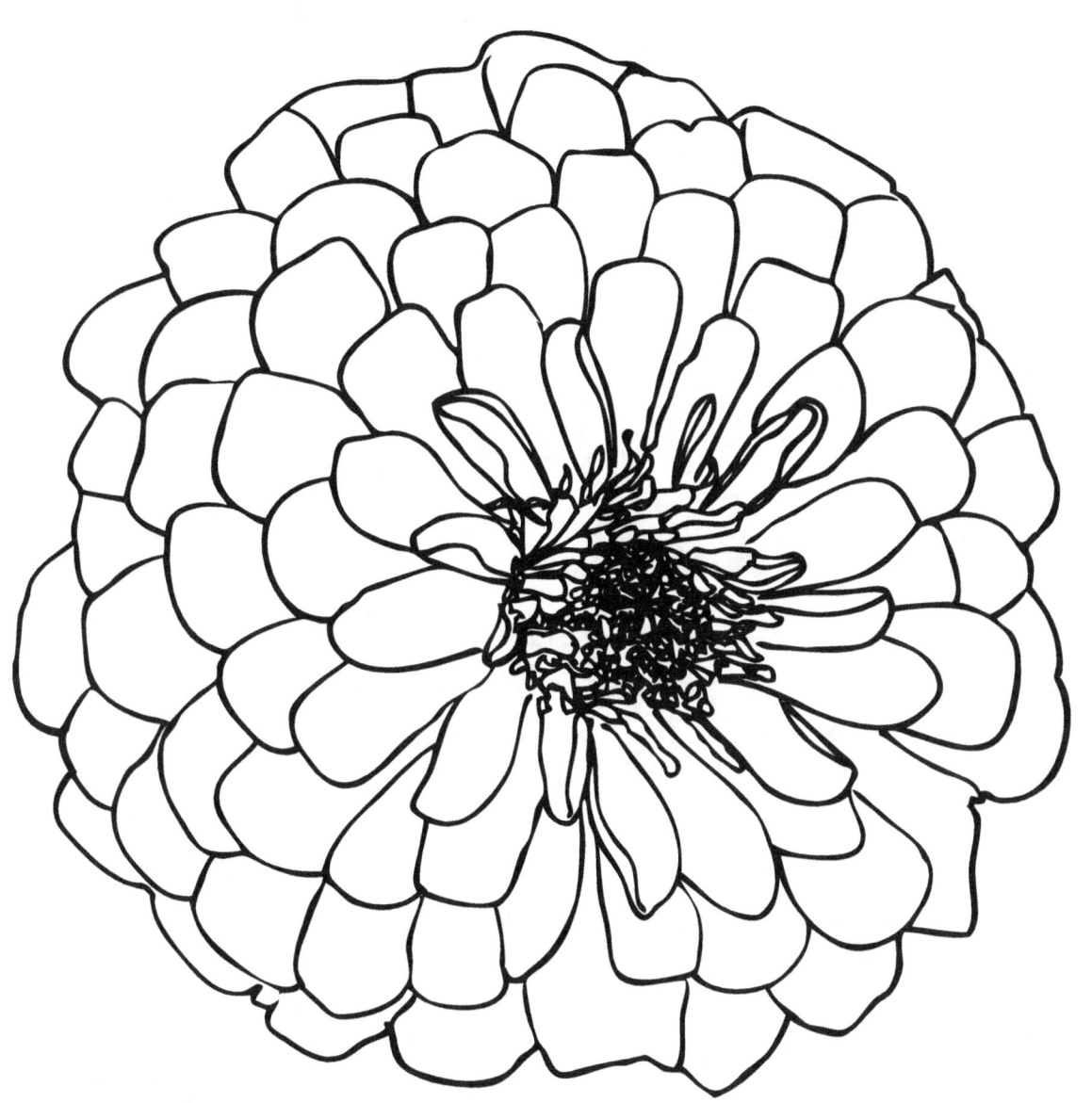

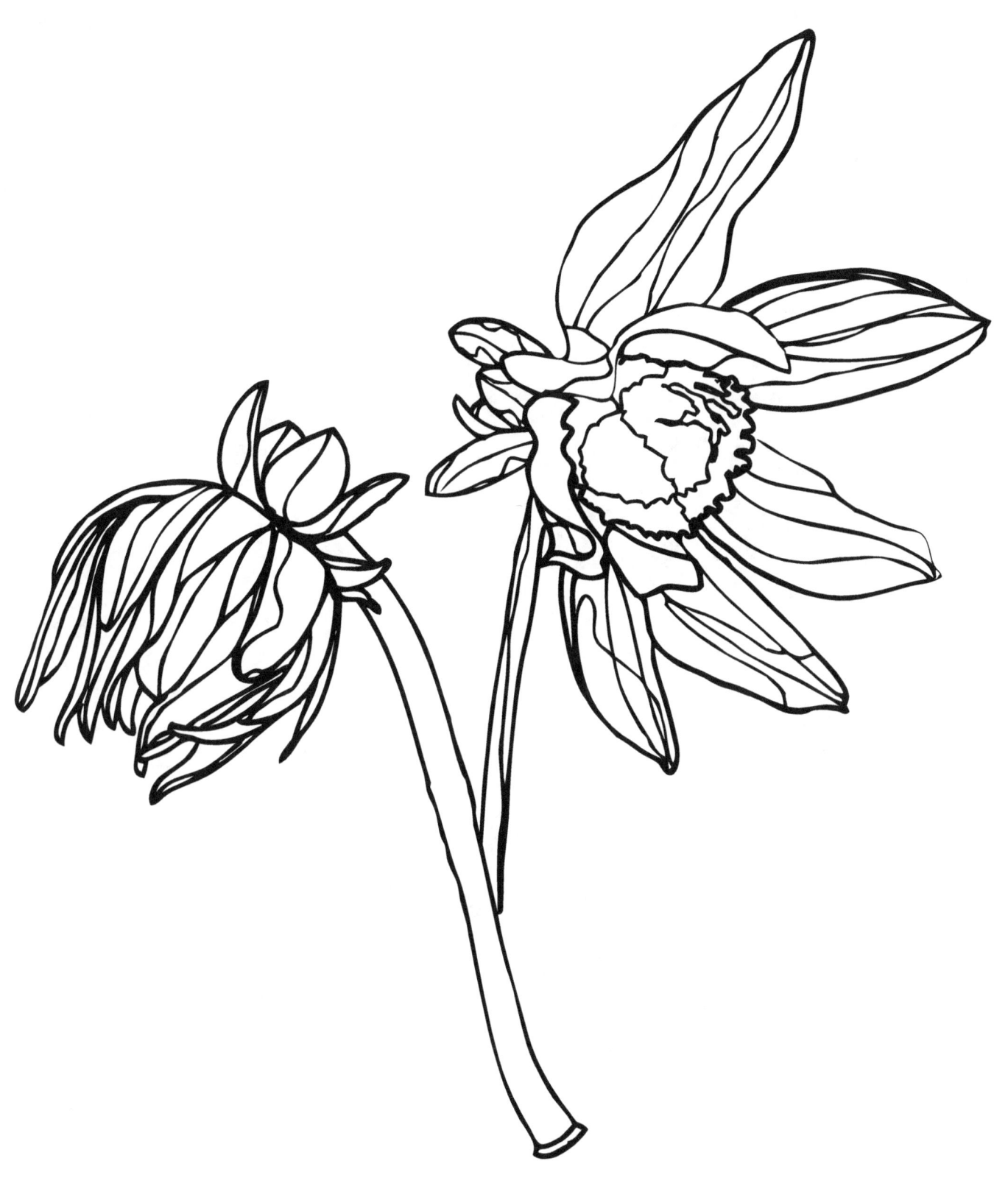

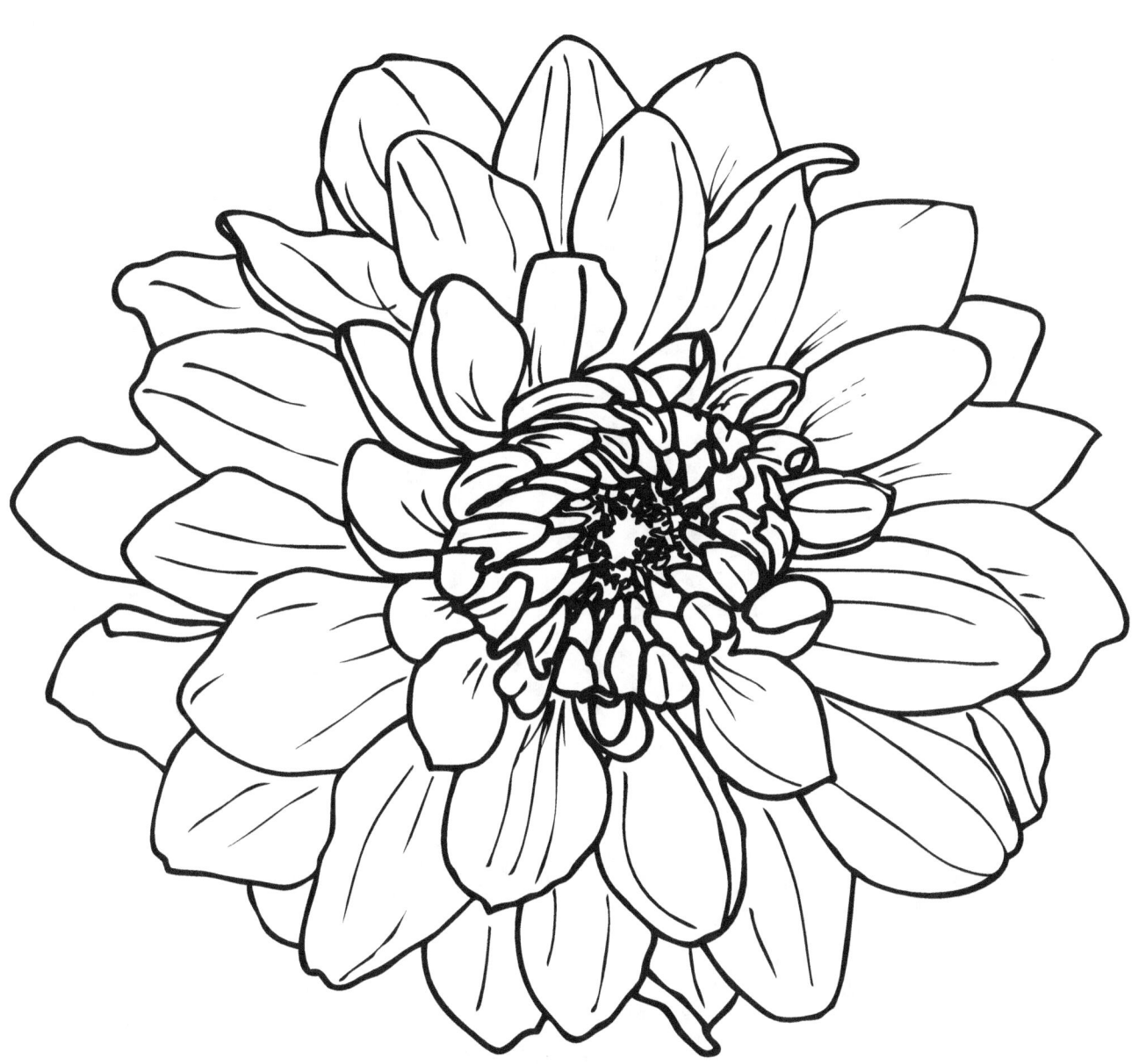

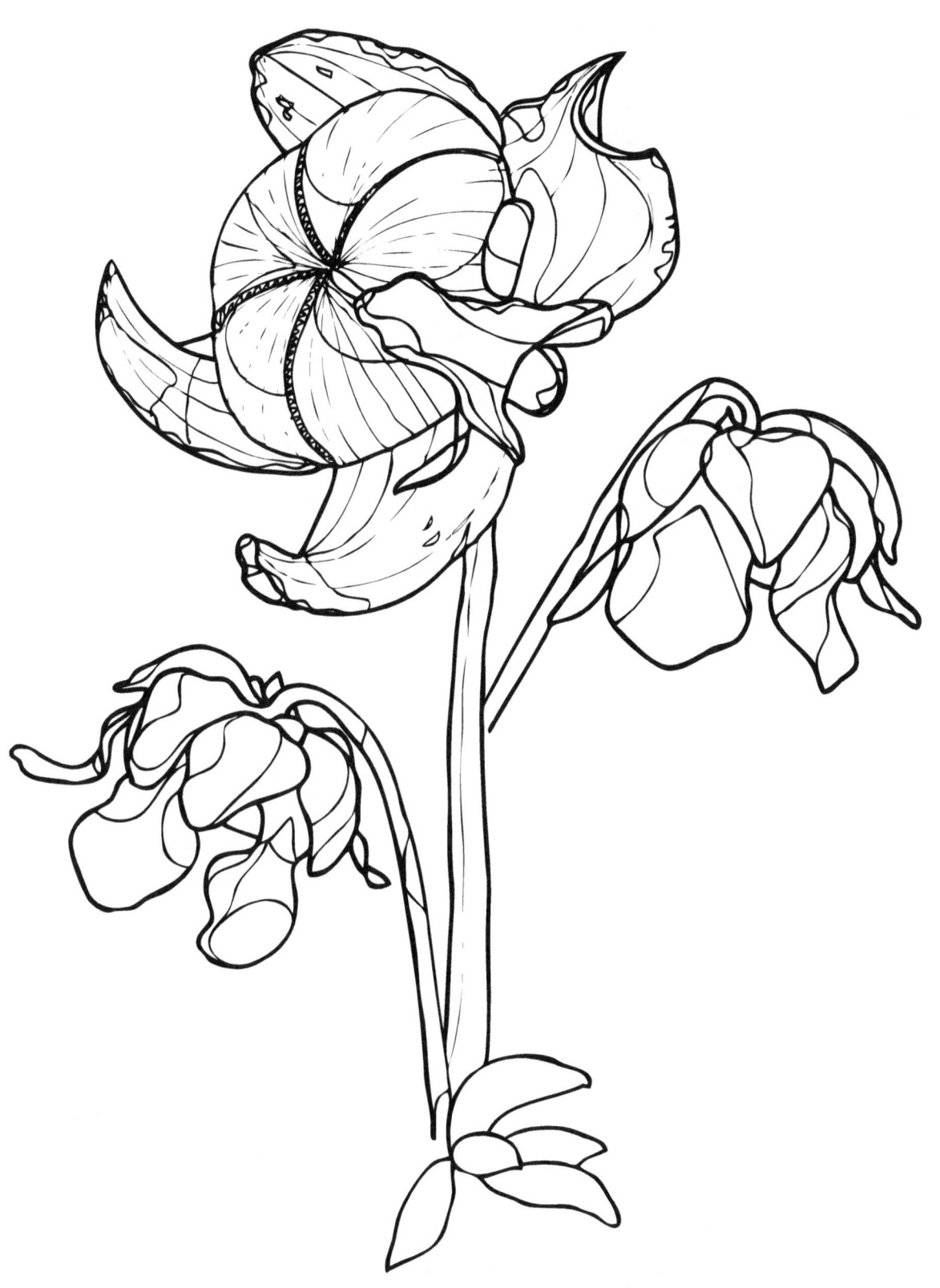

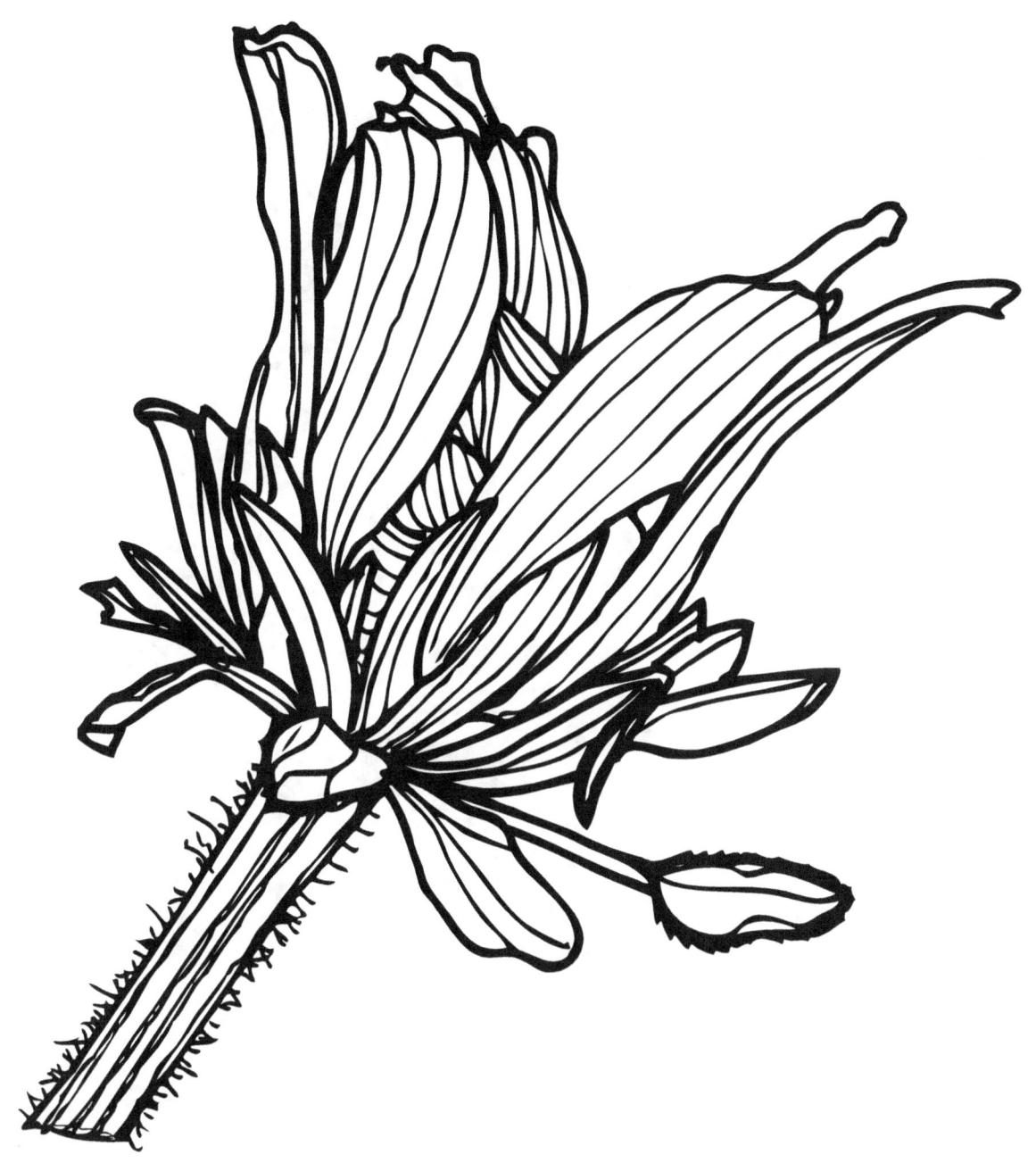

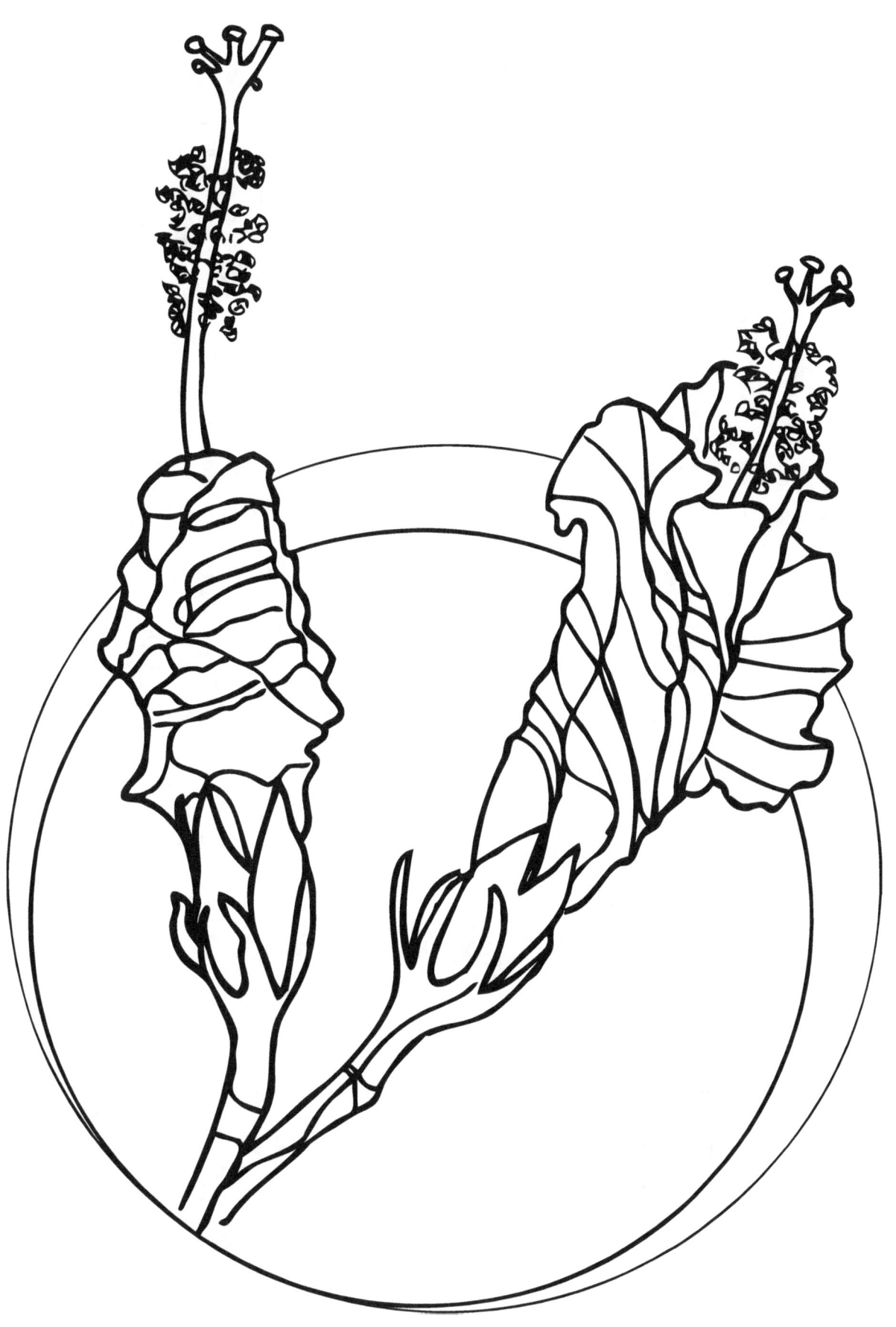

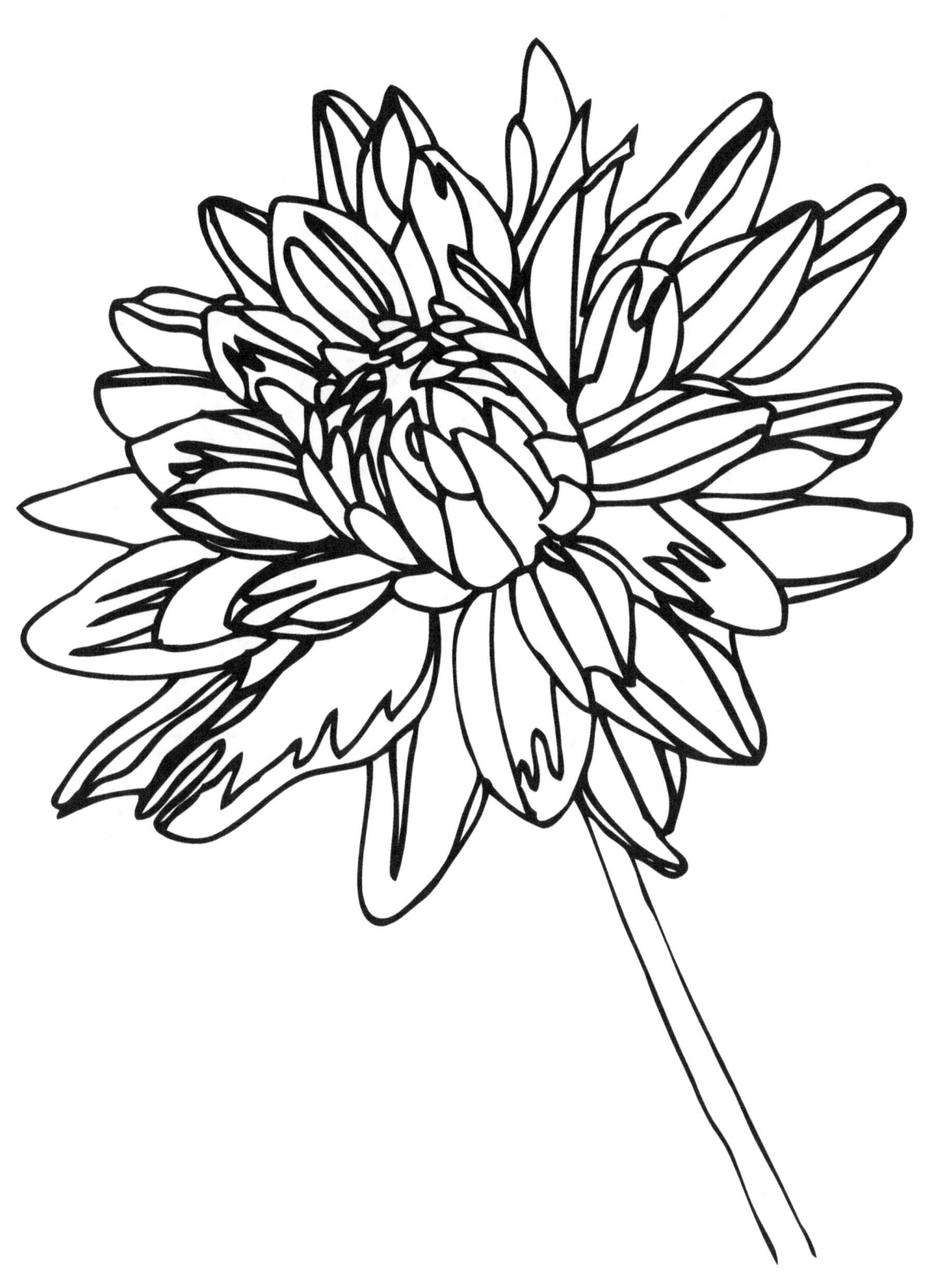

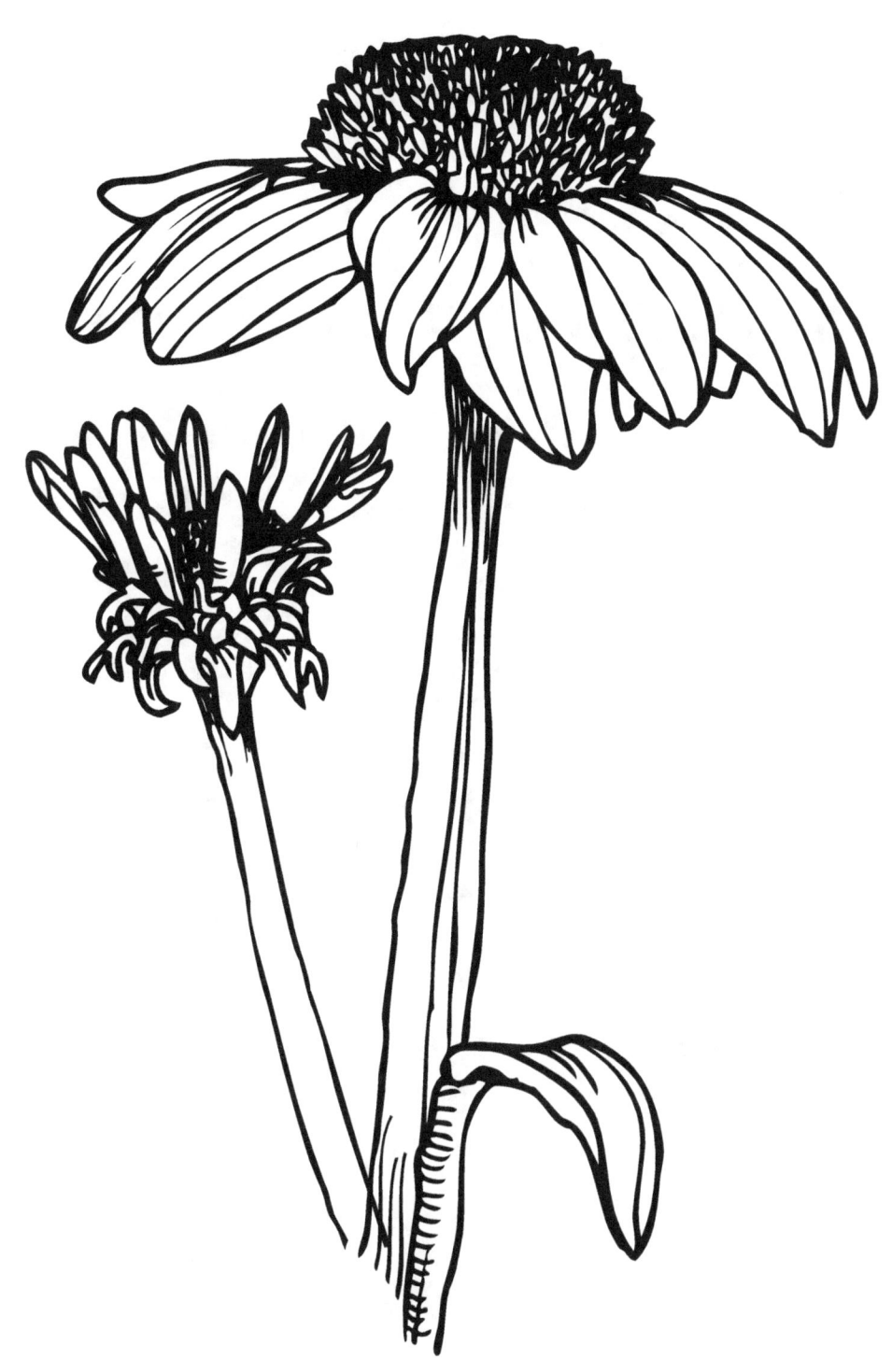

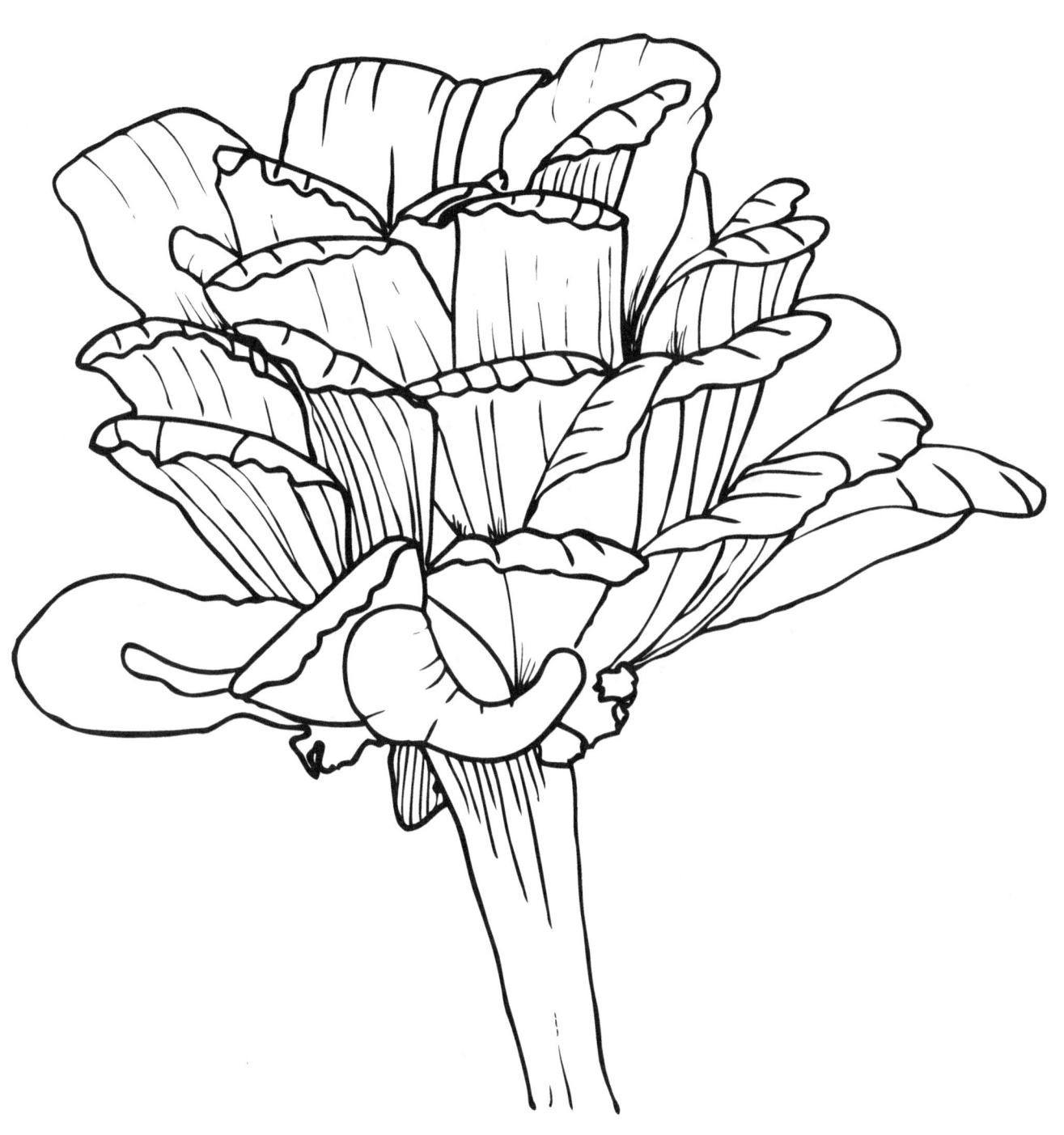

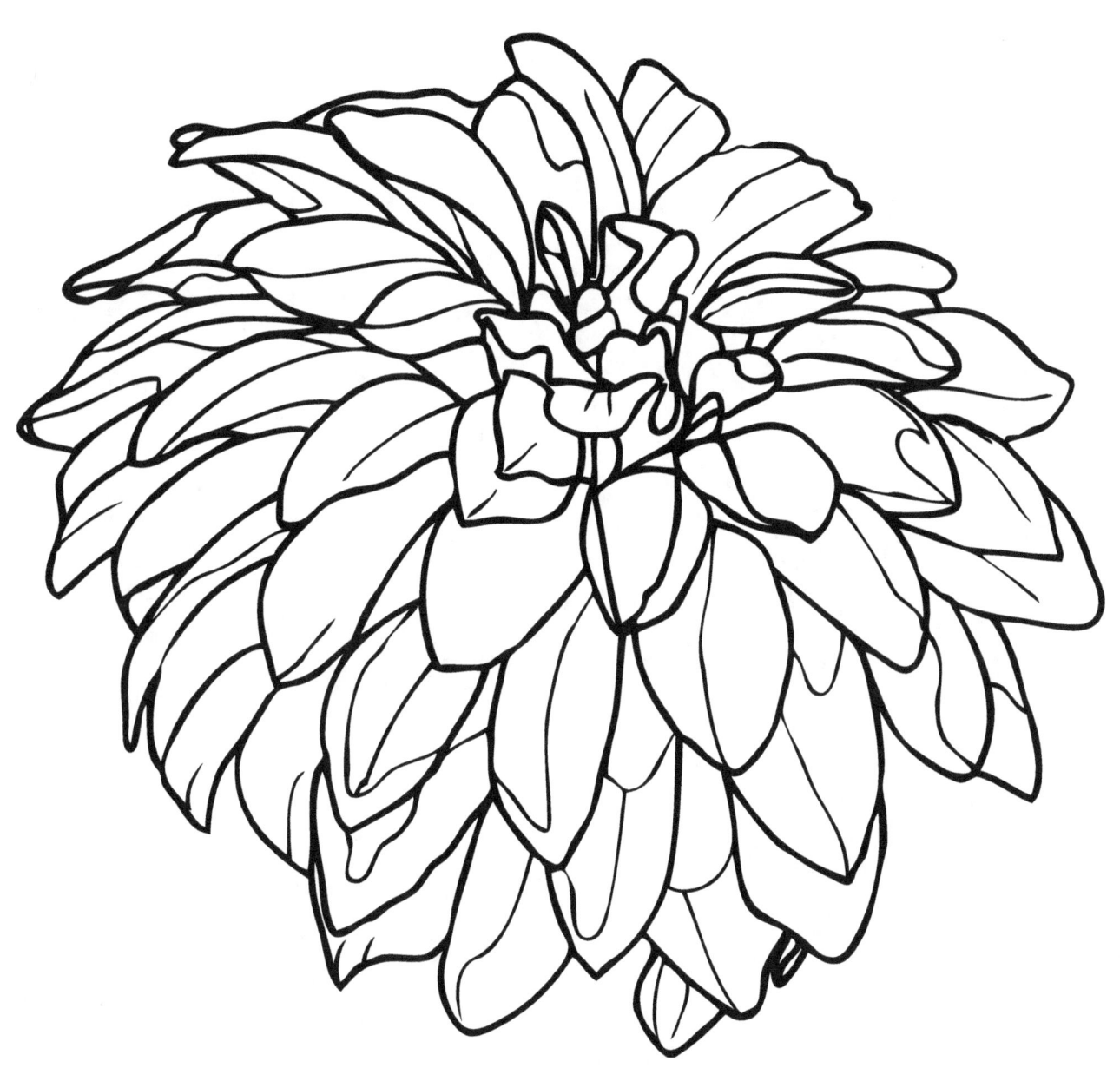

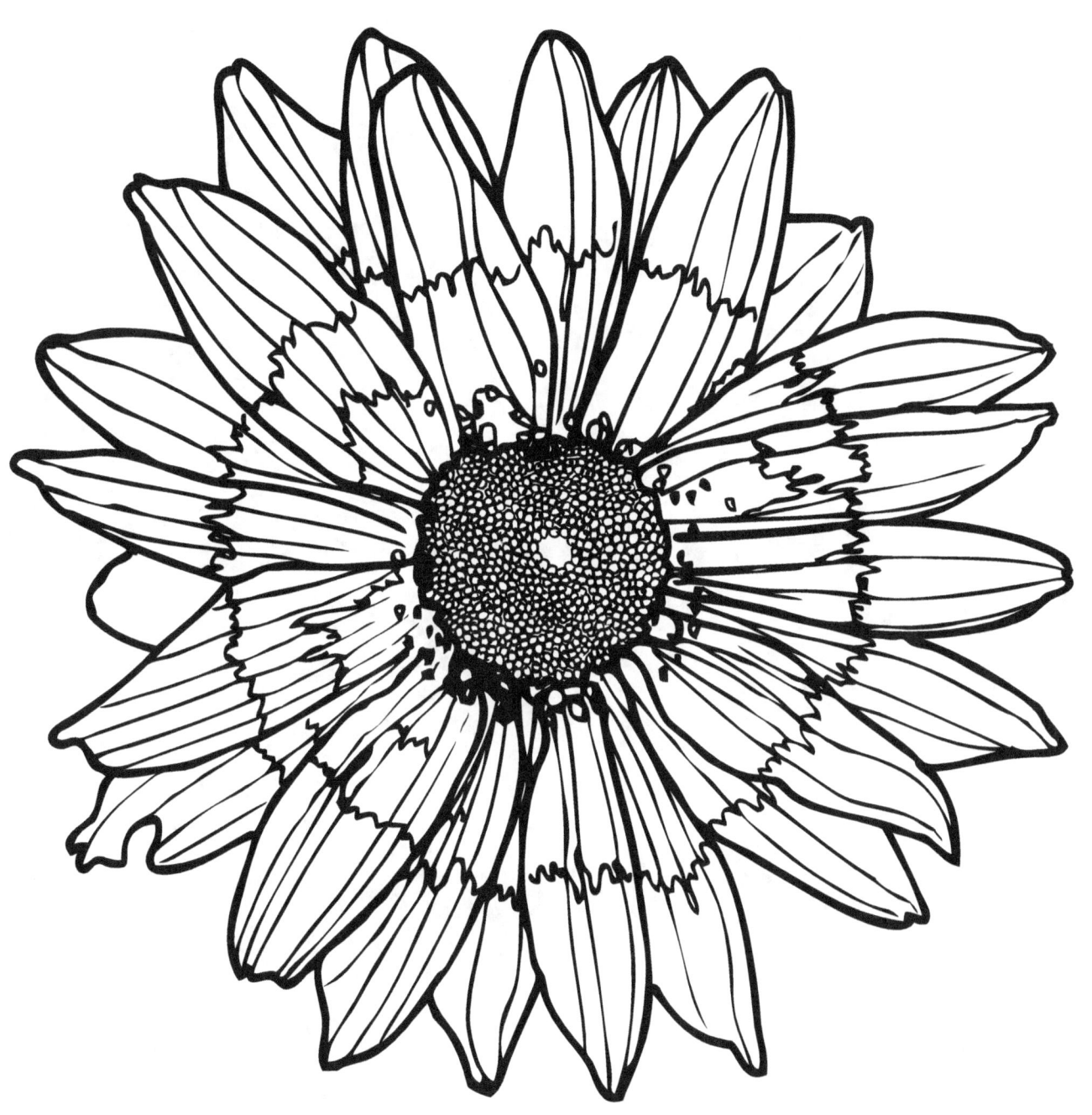

COLOR SWATCH TEST PAGE

Use this page to test and reference your colors

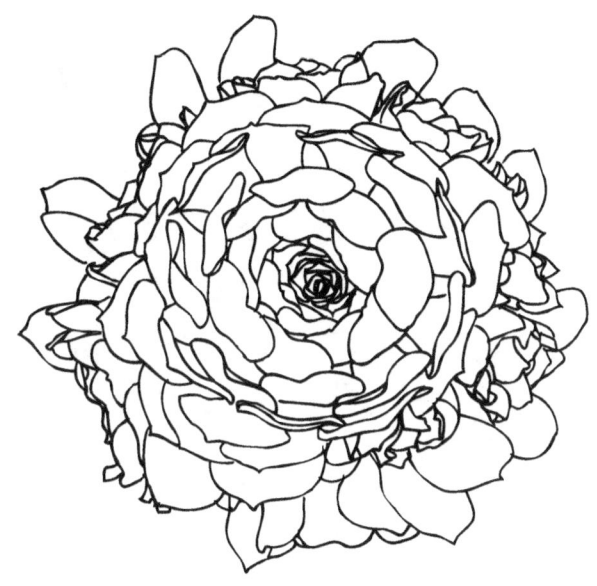

To learn about current and upcoming books,
and view colored samples of the works contained herein,
please visit the author's website at:

www.lovelyleisure.me